LEADERSHIP

IN THE NEW NORMAL

D1637251

LEADERSHIP

IN THE NEW NORMAL

LT. GENERAL
RUSSEL L. HONORÉ
(U.S. Army, Retired)

– With Jennifer Robison –

Acadian House
PUBLISHING
Lafayette, Louisiana

Library of Congress Cataloging-in-Publication Data

Honore, Russel L.
  Leadership in the new normal : a short course / Russel Honore.
    p. cm.
  Includes bibliographical references and index.
  ISBN 978-0-925417-81-7 (alk. paper) -- ISBN 0-925417-81-5
  (alk. paper) 1. Leadership.
I. Title.
  HM1261.H66 2012
  303.3'4--dc23
                       2012032092

 ♦ Published by Acadian House Publishing, Lafayette, Louisiana
    (Edited by Trent Angers; co-editor, Claire Gamble)
 ♦ Cover design by Angelina Leger, Lafayette Louisiana
 ♦ Printed by Sheridan Books, Chelsea, Michigan

*I dedicate this book to the people
of the United States of America,
to those who understand that freedom isn't free;
that it is based on selfless service to others.
And I salute those
who are earnestly committed
to lifting up all of humankind,
in our own country
and around the world.*

Acknowledgements

Quite a number of people contributed to the creation of this book and supported me through the process. I am grateful to them all:

Three men whom I respect highly, associates who read the manuscript and wrote blurbs for the dust jacket: Walter Isaacson, president of the Aspen Institute; Ali Velshi, CNN business anchor; and Jim Clifton, CEO of The Gallup Organization.

My co-writer and main collaborator, Jennifer Robison – also a colleague at Gallup – who spent tons of time researching, writing and consulting with me on the content of the book.

Editor Trent Angers, co-editor Claire Gamble and the staff at Acadian House Publishing, for their hard work and dedication to this project.

Two of my top advisors, who reviewed key parts of the text to help assure accuracy: Col. Gregory Fontenot (U.S. Army, retired) and Dr. Vicki Dunn.

My daughter and scheduler, Stefanie Honoré Acosta, who kept me on track as I bounced around the country giving speeches while at the same time working on this book; and my other daughter, Kimberly Honoré, my social media advisor.

My son, Army ROTC cadet Steven Honoré, who worked with me as my aide, typing, proofreading and transmitting information related to the book.

And, finally, two of my biggest fans and supporters, who have encouraged me in all my endeavors: my wife, Beverly, and my longtime mentor, Major General Charles Honoré (U.S. Army, retired).

Contents

Introduction
An age of great opportunity

Abe Lincoln and Dwight Eisenhower would have agreed with what General Russel Honoré has written on the subject of leadership. So would George Washington and George W. Bush, who was Gen. Honoré's Commander-in-Chief when he retired from the Army after 37 years of service.

General Honoré, one of the most-recognized military leaders of our time, shares his knowledge of leadership in the pages that follow.

Leadership in the New Normal is a short course on how to be an effective leader in the 21st century. The book is brief and to the point; it is characterized by straight talk and common sense; and it is based on a lifetime of military leadership.

You may recognize the author as the 3-star general who emerged as a national hero in 2005 following Hurricane Katrina. He spearheaded the Joint Task Force responsible for the massive search-and-rescue mission and the restoration of order in New Orleans and the Mississippi Gulf Coast in the wake of the terrible storm.

He led more than 20,000 troops in Katrina's aftermath, served as a commanding officer in Operation Dessert Storm in 1991, and was the Commanding General of the 2nd Infantry Division in Korea.

So, when it comes to leadership, he knows what he's talking about. He speaks from experience; he writes with authority.

As a military leader, he was known for his no-nonsense approach to things: "Say what you mean and mean what you say," and do it briefly. As an author, his style is much the same.

So, naturally, he defines leadership with an economy of words: the art and science of influencing others to willingly follow. And he explains how to motivate others to do so.

He defines the New Normal and makes it clear that the times are a-changing – dramatically. What characterizes this new era is an interesting convergence of elements: the rapid, nearly instantaneous transmission of information; extreme population density; extraordinary interconnectedness (and mutual dependency) of business; the rise of terrorism; and the growing ranks of the poor.

The author devotes a chapter to a concept that is fundamental to top-flight leadership: decision superiority, which is defined as the ability to see first, understand first, and act first. This ability is tied in no small way to the effective use of modern information technology.

He passes on valuable lessons he learned in the Army about some of the essentials of effective leadership: doing the routine things well, being willing to take on the seemingly impossible, and never being paralyzed into inaction by criticism or fear of it.

Having been an Army commander of missions on five continents, not surprisingly he makes some bold and insightful statements that will cause reasonable people to sit up and take notice. He predicts, as others have, that the next wars will be fought over water, not oil. He points out that a society that essentially predestines some of its children to a life in prison – via the "Cradle-to-Prison Cell Pipeline" – is a sick society that needs to examine its collective social conscience and get to work immediately to address this American tragedy.

On the global front, he advocates making more of an effort to help turn "have-nots" into "haves" – a subject that seems to be close to his heart – not only locally but nationally and internationally. He suggests that such a movement would be good for national security: "People who can feed their families and feel like they're getting somewhere in life are less dangerous people."

In a special chapter on the importance of leadership at home, he writes, "A family is a team, and teams need leaders" – that is, parents who are devoted to parenting and teaching their children.

While General Honoré clearly recognizes the downside of the New Normal, he sees it primarily as an age of great opportunity. He feels we can help more kids than ever before to get a good education – which almost always translates to a better quality of life. We can build a more vibrant domestic economy than ever before by encouraging innovators and entrepreneurs – and by understanding the true purpose of business. We can raise the world's standard of living more effectively than ever before by helping developing countries develop at a quicker pace.

All these improvements are going to take strong, imaginative leadership. This book was written in an effort to encourage and to help educate those leaders.

- Trent Angers
Editor

LEADERSHIP

IN THE NEW NORMAL

– Based on the original painting by Emanuel Leutze

George Washington and his troops cross the ice-clogged Delaware River on Christmas Day in 1776 in a surprise attack on the British army. Motivated by a deep desire for freedom from British oppression, Washington's army prevailed in the battle at Trenton, N.J.

Chapter 1

The nature of leadership

The United States of America started with a miracle.

The Revolutionary War had been a catalog of defeats in New York, New Jersey and Pennsylvania. The generals under General George Washington, the Commander-in-Chief of the Continental Army, failed him over and over. The British had burned down the American capital in New York and were threatening the emergency capital in Philadelphia.

Thousands of troops had deserted, others refused to re-enlist, and most of the rest were sick.

And every day the weather got worse.

By late 1776, General Washington's Army was literally decimated, and the few men left fought with scant food and weaponry. Some didn't even have boots and marched through the snow with rags wrapped around their feet, turning the snow red with blood when they passed.

"I think the game is pretty near up," Washington said in a letter to his cousin.

Around that time, Washington asked his friend Thomas Paine to write something that might inspire the men, something that would take their minds off their bleeding feet and empty bellies and the probability of defeat. Thomas Paine responded with his famous essay, *The Crisis*:

> *These are the times that try men's souls. The summer soldier and the sunshine patriot will, in this crisis, shrink from the service of their country; but he that stands by it now deserves the love and thanks of man and woman. Tyranny, like hell, is not easily conquered; yet we have this consolation with us, that the harder the conflict, the more glorious the triumph. What we obtain too cheap, we esteem too lightly. It is dearness only that gives everything its value....*

Washington ordered that *The Crisis* be read to the troops, every single one of them, on December 23, 1776.

Two days later, on Christmas Day, Washington sent 2,400 men over the freezing Delaware River in a sneak attack on the British forces in Trenton, New

Jersey. Washington himself led the men, through the sleet, through the ice, through the snow, with "almost infinite difficulty," according to his chief of artillery.

The enemy felt so safe from the Continental Army that they lowered their guard and relaxed on Christmas Day and failed to post a dawn sentry. Then Washington's army fell upon them.

That day, the British lost nearly two-thirds of their troops to Washington: Twenty-two of them died, 83 were seriously injured, and 896 were captured by Washington's forces. Of the Continental soldiers, two were killed and five were hurt. The 2,398 American survivors, some of them slaves, some of them veterans, all of them our ancestors, won Trenton, and by winning that battle won us a nation.

But that's not the only miracle of the story.

Washington's leadership was a notable miracle unto itself. He was afraid, and he wasn't sure he would triumph, and he too was hungry, tired and cold. Yet despite everything working against him, Washington inspired his army past their own point of endurance.

And what were they fighting for? Land? Money? Power?

No, the Revolutionary War was fought for a concept: freedom.

It takes a lot of sacrifice to start a war, and more sacrifice to win it. The men who fought the Revolutionary War gave up their homes, their lives, their families. They sacrificed everything to achieve something even more precious to them – the idea of freedom.

It's been said that we beat the British because British soldiers fought for the King and our people fought for freedom.

It's an awe-inspiring word, freedom. Freedom, as we used to say in the Army, to be all you can be. Be all you want to be. Be where you want to be, with whom you want to be. Be *what* you want to be.

But freedom takes sacrifice. Patriotism takes sacrifice. More often than not, we fail to sacrifice hardly anything for that common American value.

If General Washington had MSNBC in one ear and Fox News in the other, he never would have won that war. Our national conversation today isn't about the things that matter. We talk about freedom but not responsibility. We talk about patriotism, but not real patriotism. Genuine patriotism is a community activity. Patriotism takes something from us because we owe something to ourselves, to the people who came before us, and to those who will come after us.

As we operate inside our country, as we live and work, it's important to remember that there's something beyond ourselves. Every generation must be prepared to take up arms to defend our freedom and that of future generations. But it isn't only soldiers who keep America free.

We were born free by good fortune. To live free is

a privilege. To die free is an obligation. Each generation has the obligation to keep America free for the next generation.

Meeting the obligations of freedom is accomplished by being good citizens and good parents and good adults. Patriotism means being respectful of your neighbors and taking care of your family, living within the social norms and laws of the community. It means you get what you earn and work for.

You pay your taxes. You build value through what you do, what you create. You raise and discipline your kids, you ensure that they become good citizens. You vote and you participate in our democracy. You contribute to your community. And when the time of service comes – to serve in arms or in your community – you accept it.

While Washington and his soldiers were freezing in the snow, King George III asked the people of England to pray that the words of the Declaration of Independence would never come to fruition. He knew that if they did, it would be the end of his form of government. That's the power of freedom. And King George was right to worry.

Look at North Korea and South Korea at the end of the Korean War. Both countries were all but destroyed, forced to form new systems of government. South Korea chose freedom and democracy. North Korea chose communism and oppression. Today, South Korea's median income is $26,000 in U.S.

dollars, and South Korean life expectancy is 79 years. The median income in North Korea in $1,700 and the life expectancy is 64 years. The South Korean population is 50,000,000, the North population is about 24,000,000, of whom nearly a million are in the military.

South Korea exports food, technology and various products. North Korea is starving. South Korea chose freedom and its obligations. North Korea created a massive army whose primary purpose is to control its people and to prevent them from leaving the country. Both Koreas have a common human ecology, and had a common social and physical climate. But the choices the people made, made all the difference. Freedom changes everything.

It's easy for us to forget that. It's easy for us to be lazy about our democracy. We take our freedom for granted because we don't have bombs dropping in our back yard, nobody's taking our kids, and we've never seen a foreign soldier walking down our street. So we let our sons and daughters join the Army to defend us and our allies and leave it at that. We let our leaders yell at each other on CNN and Fox and we tune out what we find disagreeable. We let the poor rot and our cities crumble, and when disaster strikes we assume professionals will come along to bail us out.

They may not. There aren't enough first responders to keep everyone free from harm. We need to be our own first responders to keep ourselves free from harm – and the New Normal offers a lot of opportunities for harm. But the New Normal also offers a lot of opportunities for greatness and for real leadership.

Leadership itself has become a field of study that looks into a lot of questions at once.

Are leaders born or made?

Can leadership be taught, or must it be ingrained by experience?

Can introverts lead?

Does it require a dominant personality?

Some leaders demonstrate leadership, or attempt to, in everything they do. George Washington was like that. Others rise up when circumstances demand it; their leadership abilities aren't noticed until something spectacular happens.

My working definition of **leadership** is this: the art and science of influencing others to *willingly* follow. The key word is *willingly*. This isn't the strict definition I learned in the military, because in the Army no one has the choice to follow or not.

But even in the Army, and certainly in the working world, people have the choice to follow, *sort of*. To sort of do what the leader wants, to sort of make an effort to achieve the mission. That's the worst kind of follower. People who sort of put in an effort not only reduce the chances of success but they require more attention and energy from leadership than they're worth.

In the New Normal, *willingness* is everything. That's because the old command-and-control system just doesn't work anymore. Napoleon said, "Men are moved by two levers only: fear and self-interest." True, but fear and self-interest don't have much staying power. Followers either overcome fear or grow numb to it, and self-interest is tied to the highest bidder.

Today, the most a leader can hold over an employee's head is a pink slip. In our interconnected world, workers can get a comparable job somewhere else. Fear and self-interest are short-term motivators, and leaders have long-term problems. Command-and-control is a dead letter for leaders.

Sometimes leaders motivate by charisma, by their own personalities or vision. They get a lot done, like President John F. Kennedy, but their influence is short-lived. People follow, or appear to follow, because of the power of the leader, not so much because of the ideas that the leader professes. As soon as that leader is gone, his or her direct influence immediately goes away, too.

Sometimes the leader doesn't even have to leave to see his influence end; it drains away when he's caught in scandal. Leaders have to live up to the ideals of the organization they lead. When it appears they don't, nobody will follow them.

Which is not to say leaders have to be perfect

people. But, as soldiers would put it, the leader's audio and video have to match. If the leader talks about discipline, but doesn't demonstrate discipline himself, he won't have followers. Ultimately, people are looking for somebody who is respectable – not just somebody who's loud.

I am very grateful to have served under imperfect leaders, but those men and women recognized it and worked around it. They garnered sufficient respect despite their flaws and weaknesses because of their ability to deal with the criticism and act even while being criticized.

Some people think you have to be a little crazy to be a leader. Normal people don't want the responsibilities that leadership brings. But good leaders are not normal or average. I think there's something different about them in their desire to lead and in their ability to inspire followers.

If you want followers to follow wholeheartedly and permanently, you have to give them something to aspire to. Something they want as badly as you do. Something that gives them reason to *willingly* follow. When they have that, a leader's problem isn't getting people behind him but staying one step ahead of them.

How to do that? Well, that's the art of leadership, and it includes elements such as investing in your subordinates' success, embracing technology, and understanding the global environment and what we call the New Normal.

These are some of the vital issues for the men and women who want, or have been compelled by circumstances, to lead our country in the New Normal. Leaders today need a clear, in-depth understanding of the purpose of leadership. Remember, what saved our emerging country during the Revolutionary War was leadership. What will keep it strong today is leadership.

Key points

1. Freedom is not free; someone has paid the price for your freedom. Now it is time for you to help preserve freedom.

2. Good leaders need not always be at the front of the formation, but they always figure out where they are needed most. Being at the right place at the right time is what a leader does.

3. Good leaders understand the true challenge of leadership is not just about getting people to do what they want to do, but to get them to do what they don't want to do.

Chapter 2

The first three lessons of leadership

No great change comes without leadership. The New Normal is a time of change that will require leadership through even more change. Fortunately, we don't have to invent the lessons of leadership. There's a lot to learn from the leaders who have gone before us.

Many of the principles that leaders need now are old ones, lessons that have endured. I was lucky to be taught three of the most important ones early in my career.

Just as I was about to graduate from Reserve Officer Training School in 1971, one of my teachers offered a simple though profound lesson in leadership.

"I think you can be successful if you do three

things," she told me.

Well, I listened closely. She was smart, and I was eager to learn.

"First, learn to do the routine things well," she said.

I thought I had that one down cold. I was a member of the United States Army, an outfit that is all about doing routine things well.

"Second," she said, "don't be afraid to take on the impossible."

I thought I had that figured out, too. I grew up in a clapboard house with eight brothers and three sisters on a subsistence farm in rural Louisiana. I put myself through college with savings from after-school jobs I'd had since I was 11, several part-time jobs in college, and an ROTC stipend. I'd managed to not only graduate from college but also to earn a commission as an infantry second lieutenant in the U.S. Army. Yeah, doing the impossible was something I understood.

"Third," she said, "don't be afraid to act, even if you're being criticized."

Well, I thought, *everybody is going to have something to say about your decisions. Don't all leaders have to accept some criticism? Anyone can handle a little criticism.*

In later years, full clarity of what my teacher meant came to me. In fact, it wasn't until 2005 that I truly grasped what taking on the impossible is and how fear of criticism can paralyze a person into inaction.

After serving in some awful places in some awful weather under some awfully dangerous conditions and on all kinds of missions, I flew into New Orleans on a Navy aircraft and saw the absolute devastation caused by Hurricane Katrina.

I realized then and there, on that August morning in 2005, that I'd been wrong all those years.

New Orleans showed me that up to that point I had never really been asked to do the impossible and that I really didn't know how vicious criticism could get. I'd never been tested, never *really* tested.

But here were people walking in chest-high water pushing shopping carts with little babies hanging on the sides; people lying on top of their houses desperate for food, medicine and rescue; and dead bodies were floating through the streets. And I'm seeing all this as I'm about to land. I knew I was taking on the nearly impossible, and I knew expectations were impossibly high.

And it occurred to me that while it had taken me 35 years in the Army to reach that point – a willingness to take on the impossible – General George Washington faced tough situations every day of the war.

Then I remembered the three things my instructor tried to teach me: Do routine things well. Don't fear the impossible. Act in the face of criticism.

Those are the first three lessons of leadership that every leader should know. It took me years to fully

Until I went to New Orleans in the aftermath of Hurricane Katrina in August 2005, I didn't fully understand what taking on the impossible really meant. **Above:** *New Orleanians wait in line to take shelter in the Superdome before the storm.* **Below:** *Critically ill patients are evacuated from the 'dome in an Army truck after the storm, while a local resident heads for dry land with his belongings in garbage bags.*

understand their ramifications, but they've served me well.

*   *   *

Being the leader can be a very rewarding role, but it can also be a dangerous position. It's like being the lead dog on a sled team. That lead dog was selected to be the leader for good reason – because of his instincts, his skill, his ability to persuade the rest of the dogs to follow him. The lead dog has the best view and will always see things differently and first.

It's good to be the lead dog.

Until something bad happens.

Which one of the team will be caught in a bear trap? The lead dog. If the team comes to a cliff, who's the first to go over? The lead dog. So while it's very rewarding to be charging up a hill and being the first to see the sunlight on the other side, the rest of the team won't see things the same way. They'll be seeing you.

The military is a proving ground for leadership. Every new recruit is tested and examined for his or her ability to lead. We promote on performance, but mostly for the potential to keep leading the sled team over the hill. Many of the world's greatest leaders began their careers in the military and used what they learned there for the rest of their lives.

But military leaders have an advantage that business, political, social and religious leaders don't have: In the military, followers don't have any choice but to follow. Of course, even soldiers can choose whether to do things well or not, make good decisions or thoughtless ones, work hard or be lazy. But they can't just leave.

Workers, however, can quit, voters can switch parties, constituents can refuse an idea, and anyone can choose a new religion. In some neighborhoods, you can go into a mosque, a church and a synagogue without even having to cross the street.

Today, society is a lot more fluid than it used to be. In some ways that's good, but it does make it harder for leaders to channel energy and drive it to accomplish tasks, or missions – which is the function of leadership. So, in the New Normal, leaders must inspire people to *willingly* follow. When a follower can easily select a different job, a different senator, a different ideology, only genuine personal engagement with the mission and the leader will keep a constituency together.

There's an easy way to keep followers following – tell everyone what they want to hear. It's called pandering and it works, up to a point. That point is reached at exactly the same place as mission failure. Pandering leaders are just like Tooth Fairies: No one ever sees them, what they deliver isn't worth much, and there always comes a time when people stop believing in them.

Real leadership takes the courage sometimes to tell people what they don't want to hear. It requires honesty, personal investment and accountability. It takes a lot of hard work and a certain amount of wisdom. Leaders have to accept that they may step in a bear trap or fall off a cliff. And they have to work harder than anyone else.

I spent a lot of dark, cold, rainy nights out with the troops. There they are, stuck in the rain, doing what they're doing in the cold, and I pull up in my nice warm vehicle. So I climb out and I ask them how they're doing, and they kind of grunt respectfully.

As a leader, you have to remember that you might be out there with them, but it's not the same. You may understand what they're doing and how difficult it is, but never forget that the level of compensation you get as a leader for what you do and the compensation they get as subordinates for what they do is a lot different. You have to show your troops that you're willing to suck it up, too.

When you see paintings of the battles of the Revolutionary War, you see General Washington on his white horse leading the troops. That's important. Washington led from the front. At the time, generals were considered too valuable to risk at the forefront of war. But Washington knew his men needed to see him, literally see him, out in front. As long as their leader was visible, the men knew they were all sharing the same burden.

The Power of Commitment

Until one is committed, there is hesitancy, the chance to draw back.... Concerning all acts of initiative (and creation), there is one elementary truth, the ignorance of which kills countless ideas and splendid plans: that the moment one definitely commits oneself, then providence moves, too.

A whole stream of events issues from the decision, raising in one's favor all manner of unforeseen incidents, meetings and material assistance, which no man could have dreamt would have come his way. I learned a deep respect for one of Goethe's couplets:

*Whatever you can do
or dream you can, begin it.
Boldness has genius,
power and magic in it!*

– W. H. Murray,
from the Scottish Himalayan Expedition (1951)

In today's world, Presidents don't have to stand on the front of a battleship as it goes off to war. Today, leading from the front means accepting responsibility for one's decisions. It means being willing to say:

"This is my decision. I stand by this decision. And I will take all the criticism that goes with it, because the opportunities we may get from doing this will be consistent with what we want to do as a country."

When in charge, take charge. When you have the opportunity to make a difference, make a difference. And every now and then, check to make sure you still have followers.

When I was a kid we lived near a plantation. That plantation had a sugarcane field on one side of the road and a row of small houses on the other, and every house had a dog. Every now and then a rabbit would break out of the sugarcane field and get spotted by a dog. The dog would take off after it, and as he went down the road, other dogs would join the chase. Pretty soon that lead dog would have seven, eight, ten dogs running and barking behind him. They'd keep running and barking until they passed every house. All the kids in the yards would stand up and watch.

But after about a minute, all but one of the dogs would quit running, leaving only the lead dog chasing the rabbit. You see, the rest of the dogs started running and barking because they saw the lead dog doing it, and if it seemed worth running behind him, they followed. But they couldn't see the rabbit, so they stopped. But the dog that could see the rabbit, he kept running.

You might see the rabbit, but if the people behind you don't, they won't be running for long. They're going to fall off. They're going to be nonbelievers. They're going to become non-performers.

If you're the leader, you have to be sure everyone behind you sees the vision. They have to see where you want to go. Otherwise, you're going to be chasing it by yourself. When that pack of dogs took off running, only one of them could see the rabbit. The rest just followed the noise. When it appeared that there was more noise than purpose, they quit.

That's why, as a leader, your job is to make sure the purpose stays visible, attainable, and worth running toward. If you don't, your followers will stop thinking there's a reason to run.

Key points

1. No great change comes without leadership and sacrifice.

2. Good leaders learn to do the routine things well.

3. Good leaders are not afraid to act even when criticized.

4. Good leaders are not afraid to take on the impossible.

5. The true mark of a great leader is that people follow him or her willingly.

6. During difficult times the leader must be visible to his or her people.

Chapter 3

The New Normal

You may wonder why I would start a book about leadership in the New Normal with a story more than two centuries old. General Washington's day was very different from our own, and the challenges he faced are nothing like those leaders deal with now.

Look at it: Washington squared off against the world's greatest superpower with a barely trained army of farmers wielding shoddy weapons. He couldn't force his men to follow, and, in fact, 90 percent of them didn't. Washington's information technology amounted to pen and ink, and messages arrived only as fast as a horse could go. His intelligence came from scouts and amateur spies, and his operating capital depended on whether the harvest was good and the crops came in. The reason he had Thomas Paine's *The Crisis* read aloud is because many of the troops were illiterate and couldn't read it themselves.

Today's leaders live in a totally different world than General Washington did. Times have changed dramatically.

But look at this, too: Times changed the day the Revolutionary War was won. The day our new nation became free was the day it arrived at a New Normal.

Times have changed again, and again we have a New Normal.

It became new in 2001 when terrorists flew hijacked planes into the World Trade Center and the Pentagon on September 11. The world changed when a tropical storm turned into a hurricane in August of 2005 and the whole world realized the U.S. government's plans and protocols were unable to meet it.

The world changed again, and that's nothing new. The world is constantly changing; the world as we know it changes all the time.

But it used to change much slower.

Galileo proclaimed the idea that the world wasn't flat in 1610, but the Roman Catholic Church didn't get around to trying him for heresy until 1633. But in 2010, when General Stanley A. McChrystal, commander of U.S. forces in Afghanistan, made some critical remarks about U.S. political leaders and diplomats – and his words were published in *Rolling Stone* magazine – it took only two days for him to lose his job.

The wars in the Middle East, the economic and social havoc wreaked by the hurricanes on the U.S. Gulf Coast, and the Great Recession – all these things have changed us.

But only a handful of things have created our latest New Normal: extreme population density, the incredibly fast transmission of information, the rise of terrorism, the interconnectedness of business, and the growth of the ranks of the poor.

It took 23 years for Galileo to be brought to trial by the Catholic Church, in 1633, for what the Church felt was heresy – Galileo's statement that the earth was round, not flat. It took only two days for Gen. Stanley McChrystal to lose his job in 2010 after some negative remarks about U.S. politcal leaders and diplomats. In McChrystal's case, the consequences of his actions came so quickly because he lives in the New Normal, an age characterized in part by the rapid, almost instantaneous dissemination of information via mass media and Internet connections.

Population explosion
in U.S. towns and cities

Ever since humans stopped being nomads and started being farmers, we've congregated in towns and cities. Over the past 100 years, those cities have exploded in size. Right now, for instance, New York City's population density is 26,403 people per square mile and Paris houses 63,320 per square mile.

That's a lot of people packed into relatively small places, and the trend is unlikely to reverse. This is because there's a lot more money to be made in a city, there's more fun to be had and people to meet, and more opportunities to make something of your talents and hopes.

The New Normal, 1862

The dogmas of the quiet past are inadequate to the stormy present. The occasion is piled high with difficulty, and we must rise with the occasion. As our case is new, so we must think anew, and act anew. We must disenthrall ourselves, and then we shall save our country.

– Abraham Lincoln
December 1, 1862, in Message to Congress

And there's safety in numbers, most of the time. Cities become incredibly hazardous, however, when a disease starts spreading, or a fire breaks out, or the infrastructure collapses under the weight of all the people. But diseases and fires are relatively minor crises compared to a major natural disaster. When that happens, the impact frequently overwhelms the ability of the local government to handle it.

Look at Haiti. Port-au-Prince was designed to handle about a half million residents. When the earthquake hit in January 2010, nearly a million people were living there, according to Haiti's (questionable) official census of 2003. Port-au-Prince and Haiti in general were not equipped to deal with an earthquake at all, let alone a magnitude 7.0 earthquake and 52 aftershocks. The earthquake wiped out the city's ability to respond, its power, water and food-delivery systems, its medical response – everything. So when the earthquake erupted, it left an estimated one million people homeless, 316,000 people dead, and 300,000 hurt.

Had Haiti been a richer country, the consequences wouldn't have been as bad. But think of this: A snowstorm the day after Christmas in 2010 brought New York City to a standstill. What would happen to New York if a massive earthquake ripped through Manhattan?

These are issues that leaders in the New Normal must consider. Extreme population density requires

— Scratchboard illustration by Michael Halbert

The development of information technology in the New Normal has progressed at blinding speed. **Above:** *It was only about 600 years ago that the first printing press – the Gutenberg – went into operation as a means of duplicating information en masse rather than having to copy it again and again by hand, with pen and ink.* **Facing page, top:** *A sophisticated Global Positioning System (GPS) satellite high above the earth returns signals that are used in a wide range of functions, from locating oil-rich deposits below the ocean floor to locating the enemy in times of war.* **Bottom:** *All sorts of electronic devices, including laptop computers, mobile phones, and electronic book readers provide instant access to a world of information.*

— Artist interpretation courtesy of NASA

strategies, tactics and logistics that are much different than the ones leaders needed even in the 1990s. `

Information transmission now at lightning speed

It used to be that a handful of behind-the-scenes men could keep the wheels of public information turning, like the Wizard of Oz behind his curtain. That curtain is long gone. The Internet ripped it down. In the New Normal, privacy is diminishing. Hell, you can barely hope to have a conversation with a waitress without it showing up on YouTube.

Today's leaders should know that anything they say, everything they do, can be on every web-enabled device on earth seconds after they say or do it. The whole world has access to everything. In the Philippines, 7 percent of the population is connected to a sewer system, but 73.6 percent of Filipinos have a cell phone. When you hear "the whole world is connected," it means that the majority of humans can see what all the other humans are up to.

There's a benefit to that. Leaders can reach more people than ever before. In Egypt and Tunisia, leaders used information technology to get whole nations organized to revolt against their oppressive governments.

But there's a downside, too: People can spread bad or wrong information just as fast. Terrorists got a lot more dangerous when they stopped having to recruit on foot and started recruiting via websites.

Leaders can use information technology for good or ill, but in either case, the New Normal requires not just familiarity but proficiency with rapid information transmission. Leaders also need to know where to turn when the information systems break down.

I held a lot of press conferences during the days after Hurricane Katrina. Over and over the media asked me about things that hadn't happened: murders, arson, rape, theft. I was forced to put time and energy – time and energy nobody had enough of – into correcting inaccurate information. Some of it was just stupid.

A few days after the storm, helicopters started landing at the Superdome to pick up the seriously ill. Out in the street, a truck ran over a plastic water bottle, and when the bottle popped, someone yelled, "Sniper!" The New Orleans police chief heard there was sniper fire, told some reporters, and the next thing we knew, folks in Washington, D.C., and Baton Rouge, Louisiana's state capital, were wondering if New Orleans had turned savage.

The media dealt in inaccuracies because the usual information channels had broken down. TV, radio and newspaper reporters couldn't get around in a flooded city, so they reported rumors and their own emotions. And people around the world tuned in because bad information, I guess, is better than no information.

This is a fact of the New Normal. Leadership is

much more visible than it used to be, and constituencies expect a constant stream of information. If you don't provide it, someone else will.

And even if you *do* provide it, anyone with an axe to grind or a deadline to meet can publish whatever he or she wants. One of the demands of leadership in the New Normal is to make sure your constituency knows what they need to know, despite what others are saying.

The interconnectedness of businesses

Vertical integration is fading out. Very few organizations can or want to produce everything they need in order to survive. In the New Normal, it makes more financial sense to outsource whatever can be outsourced – personnel, maintenance, technology, production. This practice may save hassle and money, but it makes companies vulnerable.

For instance, a lot of companies have outsourced the preparation of payroll, their transportation, and their distribution to other companies. They do so in hopes of saving money and time. But as a result, those companies depend not only on their own employees to do what they're supposed to but also the employees of the payroll companies, trucking companies, distribution companies, and the database company that keeps all these moving parts moving. Any single person in any of those companies can disrupt the whole system.

We're so closely connected now that our jobs impact one another's much more than they used to. Regardless of what our task might be – snow removal, making sure the doors open in an emergency, getting the paperwork to the right department, doing brain surgery, leading a company – if we don't view our job as a mission with a specific task and a specific time frame tied to a specific purpose, we put our organization and the organizations of others at risk. And in the worst-case scenario, we could put people's lives at risk.

The necessity of making our jobs our missions means organizations have a clear-cut need to align their strategies, tactics and logistics. (I'll define these terms in the next chapter.) But we must also align our strategies, tactics and logistics with every other organization with which we work. Driving that alignment takes highly focused leadership. It takes leaders who understand every aspect of their companies. It takes leaders who engage their workers to the point that workers see their own jobs as missions.

Railroad Street and the growth of the ranks of the poor

Go to any U.S. ghetto and you'll see kids stuck in crumbling apartments with only their mom and several siblings, often times from multiple dads. These children go to schools where nobody expects them to graduate, and they walk home through areas that

Illustration courtesy of the Children's Defense Fund

would scare armed soldiers.

We think of America – the pundits certainly talk about America – as if there were two streets, Wall Street and Main Street. That's wrong. There are three streets: Wall Street, where the rich live; Main Street, where the middle class live; and Railroad Street – the street in the part of town most prone to flooding, with rickety houses, that gets the least amount of city maintenance dollars – where the poor people live.

And some of the folks on Railroad Street are holding grudges.

What happens when more than a third of America lives at or below the poverty line, where

The logo for the "Cradle-to-Prison Cell Pipeline" represents the shocking fact of life that countless U.S. children are essentially predestined for a life in prison. This is due to having little or no effective parenting, particularly from absent fathers; negative peer pressure; low self-esteem; and weak motivation to get a good education. The Children's Defense Fund and others are working to alter this terrible reality.

more than 40 million Americans get food stamps, where such a significant number of citizens live on Railroad Street? What happens when a third of America's kids grow up watching the antics of the rich on Wall Street and the well-cared-for on Main Street?

Two things can happen. The people on Railroad Street may be inspired to make something of their lives despite their circumstances. But more often Railroad Street gets worse.

If we don't care whether the people on Railroad Street get what they need to improve their lot in life, if we ignore their education and health, and let them rot, they become disengaged from the economy. Then they create their own economy, sometimes a criminal one. In far too many cases, the thinking can be summed up this way: "I'm going to go out and get mine. I'll sell dope if I have to, and I'll go take mine."

That creates a dangerous climate for everyone, which is why our country puts so much money (and emotion) into law enforcement. California spends $90,000 per death row inmate every year. It costs less than half of that to put a kid through Harvard University for a year.

I use that contrast for a reason: There's a direct relationship between low reading scores and criminality in later life. That's why in some of our poorer states and in some of our bigger cities, leaders are looking at the reading level of fourth grade minority boys to figure how many prison cells they'll need in 10 or 20 years. In other words, the shocking reality in our country is that certain groups of our children are essentially predestined to spend at least some of their lives in prison. That's unacceptable!

In an effort to protect and rescue children from this fate, the Children's Defense Fund (CDF) has clearly identified this national disgrace and has described its extent in a report written by CDF president Marian Wright Edelman. It's titled "A Call to End Adult Hypocrisy, Neglect and Abandonment of Children, and America's Cradle-To-Prison-Pipeline."

"It is time for adults of every race and income group to break our silence about the pervasive breakdown of moral, family, community and national values, to place our children first in our lives, and to...model the behavior we want our children to learn," Ms. Edelman writes.

The CDF report provides specific steps to protect and rescue children from the path to prison; it adds that too many children in the U.S. are "raising themselves."

Our culture has lost touch with education as a way to raise oneself up. Kids are more influenced by booty culture than they are by their schools or families. Now, I was a C student, and I graduated from college with a grade point average that was nothing to brag about. But I knew in my bones that the difference between success and failure in life was education.

I went to segregated schools and faced bigotry all my young life, but never once did I question the idea that education changes everything. There was no need to question it. I knew it was true.

But here's what no one told me at the time: The uneducated are an economic liability. My education made me more valuable to society. All educated people are. Educated people are a form of capital. Uneducated people are unrealized human capital. Educating kids does more than give them a chance at life, like it did me and so many others. It makes them functional in the economy.

The educated are a resource, a very valuable one. All those kids on Railroad Street who are not learning to read, not learning science, not contributing much of anything to their society – they're going to waste. Those kids could grow up to be scientists, teachers, engineers, doctors, all the professionals our country badly needs.

Right now, the U.S. is importing nurses and doctors because we're not educating enough in our own country to take care of our own population. And on top of that, we're outspending most other countries on education – and getting worse results.

We need to make our own doctors and nurses. Lord knows we have the numbers. There are millions of kids on Railroad Street with the talent and smarts to do it. But they don't have the education or a family life that would support their learning.

So we let a whole demographic of people go to waste; millions of potential workers – and customers – are left fallow. The U.S. and every other country need the potential of the poor; we need this very valuable resource. Developing it will take a little enlightened self-interest and a whole lot of leadership.

On the other hand, ignoring Railroad Street and its undeveloped talent is dangerous. Kids who have talent will use it. Leadership will determine whether they use it for good or bad.

An age of great opportunity

Some of the primary levers of the New Normal – poverty, crowded cities, mass communications – aren't that new. Jesus said 2,000 years ago, "The poor will always be with us." And we've had media around for a long time as well; the printing press has been with us for nearly 600 years now.

But the reach, speed and interconnectedness of these levers *are* new. And because of this, never before in human history have individuals had so much potential for so much impact on so many people. We *are* all connected.

That scares some people. It scares some leaders. It should, for that much interconnectivity is a powerful thing, and it can be used for harm. We've seen that.

But that much power can be used for tremendous good as well. We can reach and teach more kids than ever before. We can help more people become freer than ever before. We can raise the globe's standard of living more efficiently than ever before. We can extend the reach of leadership, real leadership, in ways we never could before.

An educational opportunity for young black men

I, for one, am not content merely to talk and write about uplifting young black males. Neither is Ronald Mason, president of the Southern University system in Louisiana.

Mr. Mason came up with a great idea for the education of young black men who otherwise would have had little if any chance to earn a college degree. He asked me if I'd lend my name to the new enterprise, and I readily and humbly agreed. It's called the Honoré Center for Undergraduate Student Achievement. It's part of a national demonstration program sponsored by the Thurgood Marshall College Fund and the President's Board of Advisors on Historically Black Colleges and Universities.

The pilot program was begun in 2012 with 16 students on the campus of Southern University in New Orleans. It is intended to be a model for other such programs throughout the U.S.

The program gives high school graduates with mid-range grades a fighting chance for a college education. It provides fully paid scholarships, tutoring, weekly group counseling, mandatory study halls, campus housing and meals. The students also receive monthly stipends, the required textbooks and use of a laptop computer.

In return, the student agrees to complete his undergraduate degree in education or another approved discipline that can be combined with a teaching certificate. Or, he may pursue a master's degree in science, technology, engineering or math. After graduation, he is to work as a classroom teacher in a New Orleans area public school for at least two years. When this requirement is met, all loans and financial aid provided by the Honoré Center are forgiven.

The program is financed with public and private funds, and I invite individuals, corporations and others to contact the center to contribute to this worthy cause. (Phone: 504-286-5107; e-mail: honore_center@sus.edu; website: HonoreCUSA.sus.edu)

——— *Key points* ———

1. In this New Normal, change can happen over night because of information technology. Thus, a rumor can look like reality.

2. Today's leaders should know that anything they say, everything they do, can be on every web-based device on earth seconds after they say or do it.

3. Our culture seems to have lost touch with the fact that education is the best way to improve one's lot in life.

4. Education makes you functional in the economy.

Chapter 4

The global environment

U.S. citizens used to feel we were protected by two oceans, that the Pacific and the Atlantic shielded us from the eyes of the world. But now that shield has been destroyed by invisible electronic signals connecting phones and computers to the Internet.

Now the whole world can see that the U.S. has 5 percent of the world's population and consumes 25 percent of its resources.

What of the other 95 percent of the population? Of the approximately 7 billion people in the world today – of which the U.S. has 314 million – about half live on less than $4 a day.

Of course, they're wondering why they're so poor and we're so rich. And you can bet they've also

A prime example of what can happen when "haves" and "have-nots" live right next to one another can be seen in the relationship between Israel and the Palestinian Territories. After the Yom Kippur War in 1973, Israel kept its access to shipping lanes, which aided its modernization and prosperity, resulting in Israel being counted among the "haves." Palestine wasn't so fortunate. The tension between the two has resulted in considerable violence.

noticed that the Western world, with the United States leading the pack, is consuming more than its fair share of the world's resources.

Up until the early 1990s, the rest of the world didn't know how well we live in the West. And that suited governments of lots of other countries just fine.

For one thing, the leaders of those countries feared "brain drain" – the flight of the best-educated to the West, where the jobs are better. Secondly, obvious disparities in wealth raised and continue to raise an uncomfortable question, especially among the staunchly religious: If God favors us, why are we living so poorly and others are living so well?

The question is a whole lot harder to resolve and has much worse consequences when the people living better than you are living in the same place as you. We began seeing a good example of this in 1973, after the Yom Kippur War in the Middle East.

Israel grew in size after a buffer zone was established between it and Palestine. Israel retained access to water, particularly the Suez Canal. That gave Israel access to shipping lanes and helped its economy become industrialized and technologically advanced. Palestine didn't have these advantages and still doesn't.

As a result, that tiny area of the Middle East became a case study of what happens when haves and have-nots share space, when have-nots can see how much better others are living. These days, have-nots can see the haves on any Internet-connected screen. And they don't like what they see.

Imagine this attitude of envy on a global scale. You don't even have to imagine it – it's on every TV news channel every night.

The culture of poverty exists all over the world, and so does the response to it: violence. Poverty and the culture it creates can even foster terrorism.

If you think you're not being treated fairly, if you think your resources are being exploited, if you think others benefit from your poverty, and you think they have no God-given right to do so, your response may well be to get ahold of a rock. Or a gun. Or the controls of a plane.

The morning of September 11, 2001, we thought we were protected by two oceans and large expanses of terrain. By lunchtime we realized that we are incredibly vulnerable. Worse, we realized that something we'd become very comfortable with, the airplane, could be turned into a weapon that could be used to kill a lot of people. Not an airplane with a bomb, but an airplane with an angry man on it. That realization changed our culture as we knew it. By the evening of September 11, we started treating people trying to get in our country, and immigrants already here, like possible terrorists.

That's part of our New Normal.

The prudent use of power
in the New Normal

Abraham Lincoln once wrote, "Nearly everyone can stand adversity, but if you want to test a person's true character, give him power."

That was true in Lincoln's day, and it's true now.

In the world in which we live today, the inter-connectedness of everything creates new tests of leadership and new ways of using the basic levers, or instruments, of power.

There are four kinds of power on a national scale: political, diplomatic, economic and military.

Political power is legislative. Everyone has at least some access to political power – through the vote in a democracy, through resistance in non-democratic nations.

Diplomatic power is more curtailed, more intricate. Fewer people have direct access to it because diplomatic power refers to an effort to resolve issues through discussion and compromise.

Economic power results from a nation's financial position. The more money a country has, the more economic power it can command. And economics is very powerful. We may think trade agreements are all about money – but when the commodities being traded are food or water or medicine, economics becomes a life-or-death issue.

Military power is the fourth form of power. As a retired general in the United States Army, I feel confident in saying this: *Military power is probably the most inefficient method of resolving an issue.* The world is not necessarily scared of the U.S. military. There are only so many places we can go at any given time. A nation should use military power only when none of the other levers of power works – war as a last resort.

The military theorist Carl von Clausewitz said that war is the continuation of politics by other means. I'd say *war is the failure of politics.* The day we invented the nuclear bomb was the day we could no longer afford to fail at politics. The stakes are too great. The New Normal alters war and politics, too.

The reason no nuclear country has dropped a nuclear weapon since World War II is because mutually assured destruction is a stupid idea. But these days, too many groups can get hold of a "nuke." Wild-eyed warriors, people with an axe to grind and an enemy to kill, have access to nuclear technology and materials.

There's no place you can be in the world and not be affected by terrorism. If a terrorist decides to attack you because of what you do or what you fail to do or the government you have or don't have, you're not immune to his plans.

True, more U.S. citizens will get killed this year from car wrecks or cigarette smoke than by terrorists, but we're more afraid of terrorists. That's because we're more aware of them. We see and read and hear about them all the time.

That can make us want to become isolationists. Many of us don't want to learn about the cultures outside our borders; we don't want to learn another language. We don't even want to learn the languages of the immigrants who live here in pockets and pools, and those pockets and pools keep immigrants from learning English. It certainly isolates them from the larger U.S. culture.

The desire to isolate ourselves is an easy temptation, but it's limiting. Isolation makes us less intellectually curious. The military has learned the danger of that attitude twice in recent years – once in Iraq and again in Afghanistan. Your servicemen and servicewomen have come to realize that a clear understanding of other cultures and customs is essential in the New Normal.

* * *

America's last big innovations were focused on warfare. We were very interested in developing the computer because of its ability to help us do the computations we needed for weaponry. We put satellites in the air, not for commercial use, but to spy on other countries. The U.S. Defense Advanced Research Projects Agency (DARPA) created the Internet as a means of communicating with Navy submarines and essential personnel in time of war. All these innovations were driven by warfare.

But times have changed.

Now, when we look at the instruments of national power, we should consider how to use them to help make this world a better place for us and others to live. We should take the traditional instruments of power and use them differently.

Bigger armies will not be the answer. My guess is that most military leaders are well aware of this. They understand that the military isn't the solution to every power struggle, and that the U.S. can get a lot further with economic, diplomatic and political applications of power.

To use that power, we have to understand the people on the other side of the table.

But most leaders aren't military commanders. Most leaders today have different kinds of demands and problems.

So, why should they bother to learn about other countries' cultures and languages? Really, unless and until someone flies a plane into our office, why should we care about what the have-nots think?

Because our future and our safety are not in becoming more isolated. Our future is in becoming more global. In the New Normal, we've got to be more attuned to economic and environmental change. The shifts won't be as big as they were from the agriculture age to the industrial age, from the industrial age to the information age. But they are much, much more interconnected, they're much faster, and they have the potential to affect every living person – for the better.

We can't ride these shifts peacefully if we're terrified of the rest of the world. For that reason, we shouldn't be alarmists. Instead, we should be opportunists.

Helping to create 'haves' from 'have nots'

In the late 1990s I spent two months working with the Egyptian Army, training some of their officers in certain military techniques and strategies that have been effective for the U.S. military. The Egyptian government provided me with a driver, a real bright guy with a master's degree in English. The Egyptians hired him as my driver because he spoke English, so he could report everything I said and did to the Egyptian Army. He had a dual role, and we both knew that. So I was careful about what I said and did.

Now, this man had a solid job teaching English in Cairo, but he quit his job for a month and a half to drive me around. Why? Because he made more money driving my car for six weeks than he made all year teaching.

So I couldn't help thinking, as I watched him from the back seat, that when people invest in an education and don't get a reasonable return on it, when education doesn't raise your family's standard of living, there's going to be a problem.

Years later, I watched on TV as thousands of protesters filled Tahrir Square. I watched them demand that Egyptian President Hosni Mubarak resign. They got what they wanted, and I wondered if my driver was one of the Egyptians in Tahrir Square.

Think back on all those people living on $4 a day, watching us on their cell phones. Some of them are furious that they have so little while others seem to have so much. Some are furious that God doesn't seem to have spread the wealth fairly. Some are picking up guns to even the score. But what all of them have in common is *want*. They *want* something. If the U.S. can help them get it, we benefit and so do they.

I'm not suggesting a massive socialization of the world, and I'm not talking about a capitalist Trojan horse. What I'm saying is that people who can feed their families and feel like they're getting somewhere in life are less dangerous people.

The Gallup Organization is doing a 100-year World Poll. They're a few years into surveying the whole world and have already come up with some key findings. First, what everyone in the world wants is a good job. More than peace, more than security, what everyone from a Los Angeles lawyer to a Laotian laundress wants more than anything is a good job. When people have a job, especially a good one, they have something to protect. They *have* something – and that makes them haves instead of have-nots.

That doesn't mean half the earth should be the

United States' charity project. We've seen what happens when unstable governments get their hands on a lot of foreign aid; in some cases, they use it to buy guns to shoot their own people. Angus Deaton, a respected Princeton economist, thinks that if the West wants to send aid to emerging economies we shouldn't send checks, we should send doctors and well-diggers.

Years spent in emerging countries assure me Dr. Deaton is on to something. But I'll go further: Helping developing countries develop businesses is even better. Helping the have-not countries create good jobs that stabilize their societies and keep their folks fed and progressing is better for them than an endless stream of money. And this can be good for the West's export economy, too.

We should help poor countries build their economies as a form of internal security so they can take care of their people. When a society can't take care of its people, it has not only political unrest, but the potential for tyranny as well.

So, in the New Normal, where distances don't protect or shield us, we have two choices: We can look at the rest of the world as a threat, or we can look at it as an opportunity. We can arm ourselves to the teeth and send our military out to fight the have-nots, or we can invite the have-nots into the first stages of a business relationship.

I think there isn't much of a choice. Military solutions should always be solutions of the last resort. Wars cause new problems, often worse problems. Instead of living in perpetual war-readiness, we should understand the global environment and willingly take part in it. And it's better for all of us if we hurry up and get to it.

Exporting: The key to economic growth

The United States is fourth on the list of world exporters. Nine percent of our exports are agricultural products, 27 percent are organic chemicals, 49 percent are "capital goods" (transistors, computers, car parts, telecommunications equipment), and the rest is made up of things like cars and medicine.

Nonetheless, the vast majority of the U.S. economy is driven by our "shining each other's shoes," so to speak. Somebody fixes my refrigerator, somebody fixes my car, I give a speech to a group. That's an internally generated economy, and that's good. But it won't get us very far. What separates growing economies from stagnant ones is exporting. Growing economies export more than they import.

In the New Normal, we all – every single country – have to be exporters. We all have to produce goods that other countries want to buy. We all have to be in fair, respectful, mutually beneficial business relationships with others. You know why?

For one thing, no one ever sends a suicide bomber

to kill his counterpart in a respectful, mutually beneficial business relationship. And because such relationships turn have-nots into have-enoughs.

North Korea and South Korea are excellent examples of this. South Korea, where I served for several years, came out of the Korean War poor as dirt. I mean absolutely poor to no end. When I got there in 1971, they were still using draft animals. Nonetheless, they found the energy and resources to focus on educating their children and on developing a democracy.

Now, 60 percent of South Korea is covered in mountains – not the best terrain for a country that lives on rice. So to support themselves, they produce rice in the valleys in small plots. But to enrich themselves, they concentrate on industrial production. Because of their focus on education, South Korea had the smarts to engage in, and sometimes dominate, the technological field. As a matter of fact, much of the work done on American animated movies is done in South Korea.

North Korea came out of the same war just as poor – and only got poorer. We don't know how poor because Kim Jong-il didn't want us to know. But some escapees report starvation on a massive scale, almost total lack of medical care, and an economy based on what amounts to slave labor.

China deals with its economy and population differently. China doesn't keep that big army to fight the United States; they keep it to control their own people. I'm not sure how much longer the Chinese government will be able to maintain its control. The country has a long history of peasant uprisings.

But for now, China has a thriving market-driven system because that's where the money, security and peace are. The Chinese government is in no hurry to help North Korea lift itself out of poverty because a thriving middle class just over the border might foment unrest in China.

The differences between South Korea, North Korea and China illustrate the differences in an open, democratic society; a closed communist society; and a semi-capitalistic society.

An **open society** tells you that if you want to be successful, you get an education. You work hard and the country will provide the security and the opportunity you need.

Closed societies, like the oppressive regime in North Korea, emanate from the communist culture that says everybody is in it together, shares alike, and is rewarded the same. Of course, it never works that way. In closed societies, a few people get all the power, most of the people do all of the work, and only the powerful prosper.

A **semi-capitalistic society** understands the power of money: It funds a lot of projects, keeps people happy, and permits the maintenance of a huge army. But semi-capitalistic countries have a choke hold on their own potential, and it's hard to let that go.

Cuba has a lot in common with the closed society of North Korea. Before Fidel Castro took power, Cuba had the rich, the middle class, and the poor. Castro drove out the rich, ruined the middle class, and created a nation of poor people who produce less food now than they did in the 1950s. Cuba used to be able to feed itself. Now Cuba has to spend the little money it makes to import food. Its climate is identical to Florida's, and Florida is an agricultural powerhouse.

So, how can Cuba become another South Korea? How does any economy become an exporter? And how do we in the West help them do it?

First, we've got to help the rest of the world get things like information technology and increased farming capabilities.

Poor countries' success won't result from the amount of grain we export to them, but the amount of grain we show them how to grow and process themselves. That will give them the ability to feed themselves. Kids who go to school with full bellies can learn, and a nation of educated people can grow an economy.

It can happen. I've seen it. Take Ghana, for instance. Ghana has a population of 18 million people, and it has a favorable climate. They have some rainfall and they have some arable land – advantages that countries like neighboring Somalia don't have.

Ghana's food staple is rice. If you were to go and walk around in Ghana, you would notice that they have more rice fields than anything else. What they don't have is ample capacity to process all that rice. So they have to buy processed rice from overseas, which consumes a good 20 percent of their national capital.

It doesn't take much to process rice. Just check

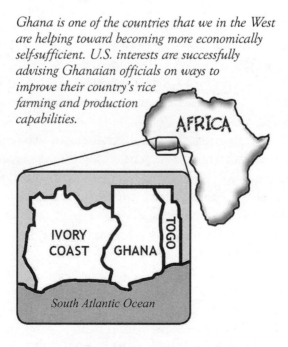

Ghana is one of the countries that we in the West are helping toward becoming more economically self-sufficient. U.S. interests are successfully advising Ghanaian officials on ways to improve their country's rice farming and production capabilities.

AFRICA

IVORY COAST

GHANA

TOGO

South Atlantic Ocean

that it has the right moisture level, shell it, then put it in a bag. That's rice processing. But Ghana doesn't have enough machines to check moisture levels and shell rice. Thus, they had rice they harvested two years earlier just sitting around, but they couldn't process it.

So some folks in Ghana sought help from an American company, a company for which I consult. I gathered and studied all sorts of information about their rice farms and discussed it with some Ghanaian officials.

We evaluated alternative strategies for increasing rice production and processing capacity. Long story short, they decided to use parts of the Asian model and parts of the U.S. model.

Today, Ghana is developing its large rice farms, and at the same time retaining its small family farms. Small farmers grow the rice and then send it to large farms which have the capability to process and export the rice.

The big farms focus on the export economy, while the small farms make sure there's enough rice to eat in Ghana. If Ghana had the machinery and the mills to process more rice, they could actually be a major exporter of this product.

Now, here's another thing to consider: Ghana has oil. Several foreign countries have come in, done some exploration, and sunk some oil wells. Those wells are going to be making Ghana some real money. But instead of putting the money in the army, Ghana's planning to put the money into developing its economy.

I think Ghana understands – unlike Togo on the east and *Cote d'Ivoire* on the west – that basing an economy on a single resource like oil can be a big mistake. *Cote d'Ivoire*, the Ivory Coast, is raging with political unrest over who's in charge and what tribes are going to lead the country. In other words, who's going to get the oil money? *Cote d'Ivoire* has the resources to be a self-sustaining country, but seemingly they would prefer to use the money to slaughter each other.

What will really save Ghana, or any country, is a balanced economy with good jobs. That starts with schools; *everything starts with a good education*. No kid of my generation in Lakeland, Louisiana, was allowed to forget it. What drove our generation was the certainty that if you got an education, nobody could take it from you. You could literally do anything you wanted if you got an education. My teachers said it so many times, I could finish their sentences while they were still talking.

Education is the key: You graduate from high school, you get through college, and you can do what you want with your life. Your way out of poverty is education. I believed it, and I'm glad I did because it's true: Education is the road out of poverty. Now, the New Normal is teaching us that education not only changes individuals, it changes countries.

School makes all the difference in the world because the education system drives diplomatic, economic and military power, and the most dynamic of them is economic power. Countries build economic power through education. And the countries that provide equal education for boys and girls are the ones that will succeed to the greatest degree now and in the future.

What the world needs now: a culture shift toward education

The number of children growing up in one-parent households in the U.S. has skyrocketed.

According to the Annie E. Casey Foundation, this is the case for 65 percent of non-Hispanic black children, 49 percent of Native American Indian children, 37 percent of Hispanic children, 23 percent of non-Hispanic white children, and 17 percent of Asian-American and Pacific Islander children.

This is a change that's happened inside a single generation. In 1970, only about 10 percent of babies were born to unmarried mothers. Today it's nearly 40 percent.

I don't think it's a coincidence that states with the worst education records and the poorest people tend to have the highest rates of unwed pregnancies. I'm not picking on unwed mothers. In the 1950s and 1960s, unintended pregnancies often led to shotgun weddings, which probably had a lot to do with the exploding divorce rate of the 1970s.

And I'm not saying that kids born to unwed mothers are doomed. President Obama was reared by a single mother and spent only a few weeks in sight of his dad. Yes, single mothers can rear happy, healthy kids who become successful adults. But the data show that it's a whole lot harder for one parent to manage than it is for two parents.

The Casey Foundation sums it up this way:

"One-parent families are more likely to experience economic hardship and stressful living conditions – including fewer resources, more frequent moves, and less stability – that take a toll on adults and children alike. When economic hardship and stressful living conditions are present, children are at greater risk of poor achievement as well as behavioral, psychological and health problems."

When I was in the Army I was sent to Bangladesh to observe the political and economic landscape. The government attached a "minder" to me, a military officer who took me around and showed me what the government wanted me to see.

One of the things I saw was a woman with a baby strapped to her back, kneeling in the dirt, breaking up rocks by hand.

I asked the minder why she was doing it, and he said because the road crews needed gravel. I asked him why the managers didn't just get a machine to do it. Breaking rocks is hard work anywhere, but in the Southeast Asian sun it's brutal. I'd hate to see a 6-foot-6, 300-pound American football player doing that kind of work for a day, so it was disturbing to see a young gal and her baby at it. I said something along those lines to my minder. He looked at me as though I had no sense at all.

"She does it," he said, "to earn money. If we got a machine, she and her baby would not be able to buy food."

Here's the point of the story: That woman was doing work we in the U.S. don't let hardened criminals do, and she was doing it with a baby tied to her back – and that child is likely to have as successful a future as many of the kids on Railroad Street in the U.S. That child may not have enough food, he may never get much of an education, and the political situation will probably be unstable his whole life. But his mother cared about him enough to break rocks to support him, and his community cared enough to make sure she had a job.

On the flip side, though that child may be well-loved, well-cared for, and well-reared, his chances in life are limited. Odds are he'll grow up to break rocks for a living. Two things will save him from such a hard life: either phenomenal good luck, or a fairly average education.

That's a fact in every society. Rich kids need an education, Bangladeshi kids need an education, Railroad Street kids need an education. Education changes everything. But to get an education, the community has to value education. In some places that requires a significant culture shift, but it can be done.

The people to lead this change are the leaders – in the government, media and academia. When change comes, it comes from there.

Consider how the public became educated about AIDS and how to prevent it. The first cases were detected in 1981, the disease was named in 1982, but it took a long time before leaders dared talk about it in public. It was a long time before anybody talked about it. I still remember the day our third-grade daughter came home from school with a very surprising request.

"Dad, tell me about AIDS," she said.

I was shocked. I was a young captain on duty in Germany, and the Army had started doing AIDS testing, but I was totally shocked that children knew about it.

But the academics got busy studying what the disease was and how it spread, the government started implementing ways to stop the contagion, and the media picked up a megaphone to tell people how to protect themselves. Hollywood started coming out with heartbreaking movies about people dying from AIDS. Government, media and academia – they brought it out from the shadows and into the light.

All that talk caused people to think about their behavior. Soon we were bombarded with information in the schools and through public policy channels, we had a very vocal Surgeon General, and you couldn't turn on the television or open the newspaper without seeing a reference to AIDS. It scared the hell out of people.

But that government-, academic- and media-stoked reaction caused a cultural shift. By 1987, the first anti-viral medication went on the market, and we got that terrible virus tamped down.

When government, media and academia work together, cultures shift.

What the world needs right now is a shift toward education. Education can turn neighborhoods from crime-ridden blights to decent places to rear a family. Education can turn poverty-stricken countries into self-supporting ones. Education can turn violent societies into viable ones.

Your mission as a leader in the New Normal: *Grow* your organization

Something else education can do is to prepare people to make the things the world needs and sell them at a profit. As I mentioned earlier, every single country needs to be an export country. To be an exporter, a country has to make things that other countries want to buy. Educate enough kids, and you'll get the people who make those things. Sell enough of it, and you'll help stabilize your country.

But sell the *right* things, and you'll make the whole world a better place. Sell the right things, and you'll make yourself and your country a whole lot of money along the way.

Companies that can take a broad view, an educated view, are going to own the New Normal.

What if there was a battery that could power a house for three days? Or, better yet, one that could power a refrigerator in Africa for a month so that food could be stored against days of scarcity?

What if that household in Africa could afford the battery because some smart person built it inexpensively?

What if we could teach computers to taste and smell? What if a computer could tell you if the milk was spoiled, if the medicine was the wrong kind, if the drinking water was toxic, if the CO_2 level in the plane was too high?

The person who makes that battery or that computer program will do a lot of good for the world. The person who figures out how to do those things will build an economy. And not just for his or her own country – for other countries, too.

Everywhere we see a good economy and good education, we see great trading partners – and a safer global neighborhood. There's a direct relationship between education, economy, governance and security.

The world's leaders need to pick up the reins and lead. If you're a business leader, your mission is not to *guide* your organization through the New Normal, but to *grow* it in the New Normal. In the old days, you might have gotten by with maintaining your market share, but those days are gone.

Hyper-interconnectedness means the world's customers are *your* customers. We all know that a global marketplace is a difficult one to navigate. But we also know it's bursting with opportunity. The more you do to encourage open societies, educated people, and mutually beneficial export systems, the more you help your own organization – and your country.

———— *Key points* ————

1. Our internal defense used to rely on the great oceans off our East and West coasts; but with new information technology that false sense of security is gone.

2. Poor people in developing countries see that the Western world, led by the USA, leads the pack in the consumption of more than its fair share of the world's natural resources.

3. These days, every have-not person can see the people who have on any Internet-connected server.

4. War is a failure of politics. The day the U.S. invented and used the nuclear bomb was the day we could no longer afford to fail in politics.

Chapter 5

Your job is now your mission

In December 2010, New England was buried under a massive snowstorm. Flights into and out of New York were delayed or cancelled or both. That should have come as no surprise. If you fly into New York in the dead of winter, you're going to see a large amount of snow.

But what did surprise a lot of people was being kept in the plane, on the runway, for hours – up to 13 hours in one case. And it wasn't because the runway was icy or the control tower was down. It was because the customs agents had gone home for the night.

And why did passengers have to wait until morning for a customs agent? Because nobody called an agent and asked him to come in.

A lot of people are working with the understanding that a job is what you do for a certain number of hours and then go home. That kind of attitude is what strands people on runways all night. That kind of attitude has no place in the New Normal.

Businesses are much too interdependent to succeed with a punch-clock work ethic. An airline, for example, depends on customs agents, power companies, fuel suppliers and numerous other businesses every minute of the day. If one of those vendors doesn't do its job, the airline can't function at the level its customers expect. In some cases, it can't even get its planes off the ground.

To a certain extent, interdependence is the nature of society, and it's always been this way. Carriage-makers depended on lumberjacks for the wood to build carriages. But in the old days, a wait of a few minutes or a few days or even a few weeks didn't have the repercussions it does now. A failure in the supply system didn't cause a tear in the economy.

It does now, because modern businesses depend so much on each other – and also because as a society we're much less resourceful than we used to be. And because we don't prepare well for problems.

For instance, the day after the snowstorm hit the Eastern Seaboard, the mayor of Newark, New Jersey, Cory Booker, was out in the streets, digging out driveways and delivering diapers. While this is excellent servant-leadership and smart politicking,

I have to ask: 100 years ago, would he have had to do this? Or would people have stocked up on baby supplies before the snow started to fall and shoveled themselves out when the storm was over?

Meanwhile, in a national news conference, Mayor Michael Bloomberg of New York City, in a very expensive-looking suit, backed by a team of public relations people, was getting snippy with the people badgering him about why his city was unprepared for snow.

Our existence is dependent on a supply chain, and that's the New Normal.

This is not necessarily a bad thing, because an interwoven, lightning-fast supply chain makes us all a lot more productive. The supply chain has made us a much wealthier society, and that wealth has improved the well-being of billions of people.

But there's an inherent danger in depending on the supply chain: It makes us vulnerable. When anything goes wrong, everything downstream is impacted.

We expect the supply chain to be uninterrupted, but anything can disrupt it, from weather to labor problems to cyber attacks.

So, every job is an essential job. That's why, in the New Normal, we can't treat our jobs as only jobs.

We have to treat our jobs as missions.

Connecting followers
to the mission

In the Army, we say a **mission** is a specified task that is to be accomplished in a stated time frame and with a purpose. A mission is not a task you do before clocking out.

If people don't understand the significance of what they do and its impact on others, they don't have a *mission*. They just have a *job*. Americans have had the luxury of "just a job" for a long time.

That won't fly in the New Normal.

But how do you make a 16-year-old burger-flipper believe her job is a mission? You can print up lots of posters that say so and hang them all over the break room. You can put the mission statement on a badge and make it part of her uniform. You can tell and tell and tell people a lot of things, but that won't make them believe it.

Workers will feel their job is a mission only if their leaders believe it and explain it.

This is something the military does well. From the first day in uniform, service people are taught how their role applies to mission success. On a daily basis we make sure people understand what their mission is, who the enemy is, how logistics or weather conditions apply. Everyone's heard the old adage: "For want of a nail the battle was lost." But soldiers live it. They know their mission in detail.

If you know your mission, you know your purpose.

In the business world, a lot of leaders bend over backward to tell their people what their tasks are, but they don't explain how those tasks fit into the overall mission of the organization. As a result, people don't know their purpose, which means they're only peripherally aware of the organization's strategy. We tell folks to flip 10 burgers a minute, but not how those burgers fit the mission of the company.

That leads to disengagement, of course, the feeling that you're just a cog in a machine. Cogs don't have missions. But when people know the purpose of their tasks and how that purpose fits the mission, they become engaged. They become empowered.

Now, employee empowerment makes some leaders nervous. When employees are empowered, they make decisions on their own and don't always ask their supervisors' permission.

That means the supervisor has a little less power. Leaders who can't stand to cede power don't want empowered employees. We have a tendency in the U.S. to promote based on personality and not on performance, to promote people we like as opposed to people with the necessary skills. And the people we like tend to be the ones who don't challenge our authority.

But you can be sure that having empowered employees is the best way to operationalize, or implement, a strategy.

The importance of aligning strategy, tactics and logistics

Every high-performing organization needs a well-defined strategy to reach its important goals; without it the organization is just spinning its wheels. But even the best-defined, most brilliant strategy isn't worth much if it isn't backed with a solid understanding of and connection to the appropriate tactics and logistics.

Strategy speaks to the purpose of why we are doing what we're doing. *Webster's* defines it as "the science and art of employing the political, economic, psychological, and military forces of a nation...to afford the maximum support to adopted policies in peace and war; ...a careful plan or method: a clever stratagem; ...the art of devising or employing plans or stratagems toward a goal."

The word **tactics** comes from the Greek word *taktika*, meaning "arrangement." In an organization, tactics are the arrangement of who's going to do what, when and where. *Webster's* defines it as "the art and skill of employing available means to accomplish an end; ...a system or mode of procedure."

Logistics is the science of movement – the movement of people, material and information. *Webster's* defines it as "the procurement, maintenance, and transportation of... material, facilities and personnel."

Tactics and logistics are what make strategy happen, the *what* that has to be done, *who* is going to do it, and *how* it has to be done. Without tactics and logistics, strategy is just a lot of hot air.

When the snowstorm hit New York City, Mayor Bloomberg could have used the help of the National Guard, but he didn't ask for it. The city had the wrong tactics.

The Guard should have been pre-positioned in case the snowstorm outstripped the city's ability to respond, but they weren't. The city had the wrong logistics.

In the end, whatever strategy New York City had for dealing with a massive snowstorm on a weekend during a national holiday fell to hell and a lot of people suffered because of it.

You have to have alignment among your strategy, your tactics and your logistics or your mission is in real trouble. BP's oil spill in the Gulf of Mexico in 2010 is a prime example: There was no alignment among the company's strategy for containment, tactics for responding to the oil, and logistics for dealing with the oil that was pouring out of the well. A lot of senior leaders were wanting to play checkers when they should have been playing chess, so to speak.

That lack of alignment has no place in the New Normal, if for no other reason than there's so little time. Decisions have to be made fast and they have to fit the problem on the ground. Leaders have to have a clear description of the what, why and how

– AP Photo / U.S. Coast Guard

Fire boat response crews battle the blazing remnants of the offshore oil rig Deepwater Horizon in the Gulf of Mexico on April 21, 2010. The blowout led to one of the worst environmental disasters ever recorded in the U.S. and to a colossal public relations nightmare for British Petroleum (BP) oil company. The damage to the Gulf and its coast could have been lessened if BP would have more effectively aligned its strategy, tactics and logistics for containing the massive amount of oil that escaped from its well.

of operationalizing strategy.

A leader's job is to decide what needs to be done, who should do it, how they should do it, and then supervise the way it's done. That does not mean leaders are the only ones with brains in their heads. Subordinates have some ideas, too – sometimes the best ideas.

In most cases, an organization's leaders aren't the ones making contact with the customers or the constituency; it's the frontline workers. In the New Normal, companies are a lot better off if their people understand what has to be done and why, and if they have some leeway to make some decisions regarding the how. Frontline employees are the ones who operationalize the strategy of the organization, and most of the time they don't have a supervisor standing over them, telling them how to do it. That's a good thing. People aren't plow horses, needing to be bossed every second.

But, more importantly, people can't internalize the what, why and how if they aren't allowed a little self-agency to do it. Internalizing what, why and how connects people to the purpose of the organization.

Easier said than done, I know. The secret to this, the secret to empowering workers to fulfill their mission, is coming to grips with the fact that to lead, leaders must clearly explain the mission. Remember, only the lead dog can see the view ahead. Everyone else is looking at his tail. Show the pack what you see and they're more likely to follow.

Managing perceptions
and dealing with the media

One of the best lessons I learned from Hurricane Katrina came from an observation made by my boss. He saw me doing a news interview one morning shortly after the hurricane.

"Russ, remember, the Army is an outdoor sport. Do all your future interviews outdoors," he said.

And from that day on, that's what I did. I never would do an interview inside because I wanted people to see what I saw. I needed to literally point to and show things happening.

Bear in mind, however, that leaders can't show the mission if they don't walk the walk. If leaders are taking enormous bonuses during a round of layoffs, they will create a lot of doubt in their workforce. The top has to be in sync with the bottom of the organization or workers won't believe in their company's mission. Until the 1980s, leaders had the luxury of insulating themselves from the rank-and-file. People didn't have much information; they didn't know what was going on at the top of the organization.

Now, of course, they do. And in big organizations, or small organizations with a big impact, everyone else on earth knows what's happening at the top. When something unexpected happens, attention can be a serious problem. If that serious problem is also interesting, look out! The media is chock-full of what's going wrong, who's at fault, and whose head is going to roll.

In bad times, followers need to see leaders leading, but so does the public. Leaders must be proactive. They should be at the scene and give firsthand accounts of what's happening. People are a lot more understanding when they see the leader as an action figure rather than a figurehead.

A leader can't be an action figure in a boardroom and absent on the plant floor. Remember Tony Hayward, the former CEO of BP until BP dumped millions of gallons of oil in the Gulf of Mexico? Hayward may have been a competent geologist, but I doubt he ever had a class in media relations. Otherwise, he wouldn't have spent weeks taking one foot out of his mouth just long enough to get the other foot in.

The first chance he got for some time off, he went back to England to watch his yacht sail in a race. This scene didn't set well with the people on the Gulf Coast, it didn't fit with BP's corporate image, and it certainly didn't help any BP worker feel his or her job was a mission. Tony Hayward failed in his effort to lead in this crisis.

My former boss, President George Bush, had a different problem – doing the right thing but seemingly being unconcerned with the public's perception of it. President Bush took a lot of heat for not visiting New Orleans sooner after Hurricane Katrina. In his

White House photo by Eric Draper

My Commander-in-Chief, President George W. Bush, and I discuss evacuation issues in the aftermath of Hurricane Katrina on September 5, 2005, as we head for the Emergency Operations Center in Baton Rouge. The President made the decision not to land in New Orleans immediately after the hurricane because he did not want to distract from the rescue operation nor use up any of the available troops to provide him with security. It was a good decision, though some critics felt he should have showed up in New Orleans – for the sake of appearance. His decision was the right one and was in the overall best interest of the rescue operation.

book, he notes that if he had to do it all over again, he would have landed the day after the storm in Baton Rouge, where the Emergency Operations Center was set up, some 80 miles northwest of New Orleans.

Yet he had a good reason for doing a fly-over rather than landing in New Orleans. Presidents require a lot of security and communication channels, and he felt that showing up in New Orleans when all hell was breaking loose would have disrupted the ground operations. He thought he was doing the right thing by not overburdening the security system. It was a good, rational decision, but it backfired. Unlike Tony Hayward, President Bush did the right thing, though he didn't manage perceptions so well.

Mayors Booker and Bloomberg faced the same issue after the snowstorm. Booker was seen helping people scoop their cars out of drifts. Bloomberg held a press conference in an expensive suit and told people to quit yelling at him. His effort to communicate didn't work. It wasn't even leadership.

People are looking for leaders who are clearly aligning strategy, tactics and logistics. That's as true in business as it is in politics. Leaders have to get those three things right. That's their mission.

Then leaders have to communicate that alignment. Luckily, there's a formula for it. It's called "the Zumwalt Rules."

Admiral Elmo Zumwalt was Commander of U.S. Naval Forces for a while during the Vietnam War.

Among other things, that war taught him how to communicate with the public. One thing he advised was to never miss the opportunity to talk about what's important to you when you're dealing with the press. But do it in the following way:

First, regardless of what the first question is, say whatever you believe is most important to you and your organization. Then, no matter what the second question is, you tell them the second most important thing. For the third question, you repeat the answer to number one. Zumwalt seemed to feel that what the press wants to hear doesn't matter; what the American public needs to know is what matters.

During Hurricane Katrina, there were a lot of different reports coming out in the media – and many of them were inaccurate. The Zumwalt Rules helped me tell the public what we were doing to make people safe.

Fortunately, most leaders, at least in business, don't have to deal with the media. But the Zumwalt Rules come in handy when communicating strategy to followers.

That's what leading is – getting people to willingly do what must be done to complete the mission. So, no matter what's going on, leaders need to talk about the most important thing first, the second-most important thing second, and the most important thing third.

Keeping the Zumwalt Rules in mind helps during

day-to-day operations. But they are incredibly useful during catastrophes. And believe me, sooner or later something will go wrong in every organization.

And few organizations are ever ready for it.

When the plan makes contact with the reality

We have an old axiom in the Army: The plan never survives contact with the enemy. Take the snow plan that the City of New York had, take the BP plan for dealing with a runaway well, take the financial system's plan for a shakeup in the system. None of them were any good. They were all out of touch with reality.

I'm not saying a leader shouldn't plan. Goodness, no! I think everyone should be ready for what's coming down the pike. But leaders have to keep their plans updated. The plans will give you the data and the information you need for the moment a situation happens. But the data on hand are not always going to fit the situation. So if you're going to use that plan on short notice, you've got to figure out which parts of the plan you're going to throw out.

This is especially true in an emergency. In a disaster, there are rules you're going to have to break, because when you make a plan, you make assumptions. When something bad happens, you have to go back and validate whether those assumptions are still valid.

For instance, BP assumed it would have 500 gallons of oil coming out a day. It didn't – it had hundreds of thousands of gallons pouring out. BP needed to update its plan immediately, but the company didn't have the leadership or know-how to do it.

Of course, BP knew that the worst *could* happen. Anyone – and everyone in the oil industry – could imagine an unstoppable well spewing a toxic substance into a fragile ecosystem.

So, if anybody could have foreseen the worst, why didn't BP prepare for the worst? Why didn't New York have the National Guard pre-positioned in case the snowstorm overwhelmed the city? Why didn't the leaders of Newark, New Jersey, spend time in the fall urging residents to put snow tires on their vehicles?

It's because people rarely prepare for the worst-case scenario. In the New Normal – a world rich in litigation – that's short-sighted. Businesses are so closely connected and cities are so densely populated that even small problems can have big consequences. Hurricane Katrina would have caused a lot of damage even if New Orleans had been prepared for it. But New Orleans wasn't, and what would have been a bad problem turned into a major catastrophe.

We in the U.S. have to not only recognize the worst-case scenario, but we need to be able to plan and take actions that help mitigate it. Right now, that's not happening – and this failure to act could be lethal in a country with millions of people living in relatively small areas.

Yet, many people are absolutely sure a professional will save them. And they really do expect to be saved.

American resiliency has changed. I lived in a cold climate only a couple of times in my life, in Germany and in Kentucky. Those two places get a lot of snow and ice. In Germany, I put studded snow tires on my 1982 Buick Century every winter. When we lived in Kentucky, I put snow tires on my front-wheel-drive Honda. I thought it was obvious: When it snows a lot you need snow tires or tire chains.

How many New Yorkers do you think put snow tires or chains on their cars?

Hell, Cubans are in better shape than New Yorkers when disaster happens. Cubans don't have anything like the Federal Emergency Management Agency (FEMA). And they don't have insurance. So when it's time to evacuate before a storm – and I've witnessed this myself – they willingly go and they take with them their stove, their bed, their television and their refrigerator. When the water goes down, they know they can return to their houses, but there's no way to replace ruined stuff. If they leave those items behind, they're out of luck because the government isn't going to send a check.

Putting on snow tires or chains doesn't seem like much effort. Putting a Red Cross emergency kit in your closet seems like even less effort. It does take a little money though: Snow tires cost a few hundred dollars, and a three-day emergency kit from the Red Cross runs about $50. But even that small investment strikes a lot of people as too much work and too much money.

So, can it be any surprise that big organizations seem to think the same way?

An ounce of prevention is worth a pound of cure

Two days before Hurricane Katrina hit, the New Orleans Saints had a football game. The day before Hurricane Gustav hit, LSU had a football game. Neither game was called off – the economic consequences were considered too severe – even though the city was being evacuated at the same time!

Talk about false economy!

Leaders in the New Normal have to weigh the costs – but they have to recognize the *actual* costs. It's a whole lot more expensive to fix a problem than prevent it, and the cost of picking up the pieces has to be considered in the planning stage.

This would all be easier and less expensive if Americans would take a little responsibility for themselves, become more resilient. Leaders can't assume that will happen, however, because people are more and more dependent on the government.

Meanwhile, government is spending billions of tax dollars on counterterrorism security and overlooking family security for things like storms and floods.

You're a lot more likely to be killed by a mosquito than a terrorist, yet the 2012 Homeland Security budget was $56.3 billion and federal mosquito-control programs were losing funding.

We ignore the probable-worst if it's boring, if it takes a little effort to prepare for, or if it is expensive – like mosquito-borne illnesses. And we panic over the improbable-worst if it's dramatic. In neither case do we do what we ought to do.

But one function of leadership is to get people to do what they ought to do, even when they don't want to. Leadership fails to do this when its confidence exceeds its competence. In the New Normal, there can't be a big gap between confidence and competence. Things happen fast and to a lot of people, and the consequences can be very, very substantial.

To get the right outcomes, however, to make the right decisions at the right time, we need more than leadership. We need decision superiority.

Key points

1. A lot of people still have the understanding that a job is what you do for a certain number of hours and then go home. This attitude has no place in the New Normal. Your job is now your mission.

2. Today's businesses are much too interdependent to succeed with only a punch-the-clock work ethic.

3. If people don't understand the significance of what they do and their work's impact on others, they don't have a mission.

4. We expect the supply chain to be uninterrupted, but anything can disrupt it – from weather to labor problems to cyber attacks.

5. Workers will feel their job is a mission only if their leaders believe it.

Chapter 6

Decision superiority

General George Washington's army wasn't well-trained or well-equipped, and my guess is that they would have all preferred to be home for Christmas rather than stuck in a freezing military camp.

Yet Washington chose Christmas Day to launch his attack on the British because he knew they would be in their quarters celebrating the holiday.

You could say Washington had the element of surprise. But he had more than that: He had decision superiority. Rather, he *took* decision superiority.

The British had the same opportunity, and they were working under the same conditions. But they didn't see first, understand first and act first. Washington did, thus he *took* decision superiority.

Whoever sees first, understands first and acts first has decision superiority – and it makes all the difference.

That's why the first three principles of leadership are so important – doing the routine things well, being willing to take on the impossible, and not fearing criticism. These elements put leaders in a position to take decision superiority when the opportunities arise.

When the routine things are done well – when the paperwork is filled out and filed, when the plant is inspected and the machines are operating properly, when the pay stubs have the right numbers on them every month – the leader is able to give his undivided attention to the task at hand.

Doing the routine things well is essential to success. It helps minimize mistakes. When routines are well-established no one has to guess what they're supposed to do; everyone knows his or her role and understands the overall mission. Your team is trained, equipped and ready to roll. You can act on – not react to – the environment.

Being willing to take on the impossible is a big part of what allows leaders to take decision superiority. Many, many opportunities are lost because opportunity is often mistaken for trouble.

What halts some leaders who otherwise would have decision superiority is fear of criticism. Such leaders may have their strategy, tactics and logistics

The Man
In The Arena

It's not the critic who counts, not the man who points out how the strong man stumbled, or where the doer of deeds could have done them better.

The credit belongs to the man who is actually in the arena, whose face is marred by dust and sweat and blood, who strives valiantly, who errs and comes up short again and again, who knows the great enthusiasms, the great devotions, and spends himself in a worthy cause.

Give credit to the man who, at best, knows in the end the triumph of high achievement, and who, at the worst, if he fails, at least fails while daring greatly, so that his place shall never be with those cold and timid souls who know neither victory nor defeat.

–Theodore Roosevelt

in perfect order, and they may have the guts to take on the impossible – but still they fear the response of their colleagues and bosses. They hesitate, they second-guess, they pace and bite their nails – not because they fear losing the battle, but because they fear criticism. In so doing, they lose the advantage. As Aristotle said:

"Criticism is something we can avoid easily by saying nothing, doing nothing, and being nothing."

There simply isn't time for doing nothing in the New Normal. Change occurs much faster these days. Decision superiority – seeing first, understanding first and acting first – enables the leader and the organization to not only manage change, but to lead the way to change.

Seizing the future: Being ready when opportunity knocks

Think about Microsoft. Bill Gates didn't invent the computer and he didn't invent software. But Microsoft was the first company to see that relatively inexpensive and reliable software had a business application. Microsoft understood that if enough computers ran Microsoft products, the business world would think in Microsoft's terms by default.

And Microsoft, far more than any other software company, was willing to act fast to get their products designed, packaged and shipped.

In 1982, Microsoft started work on a PC operat-

Microsoft chairman Bill Gates demonstrates a new product at a launch event in 2004. His company came out with the Windows operating system in 1985, and 10 years later 80% of the computers in the world were using the program. Gates, like many of the world's most noted leaders, demonstrated decision superiority; he was ready to capitalize on this unique business opportunity when it presented itself.

ing system.

In 1985, the company came out with Windows (which was roundly criticized, by the way).

By 1988, Microsoft was the world's biggest software manufacturer.

By 1995, 80 percent of the world's computers were running on Microsoft.

By 2010, Microsoft was selling seven copies of Windows 7 every second – the fastest-selling operating system ever.

Microsoft took decision superiority because the company saw first, understood first and acted first. The ability to do this isn't limited to companies like Microsoft. Other businesses, large and small, have opportunities similar to what Microsoft's leaders had. The key point here is that successful leaders are ready when the opportunities present themselves.

We tend to think that people like Bill Gates or George Washington have special insight, that they're better able to predict the future. I don't think that's true. I think that leaders like these are just more prepared to seize the opportunity. They do routine things well, they'll take on the impossible, and they don't fear criticism. So when the time comes to make a decision, they're simply more ready, willing and able to do so.

In every period of our country's history, our leaders have succeeded in taking on the impossible and turning it into reality. Washington did the impossible in defeating the British on that cold Christmas Day. Charles Lindbergh did the impossible when he crossed the ocean alone in a single-engine airplane. My generation grew up watching *Star Trek* on TV, then watched astronauts rocket off to the moon and to distant planets in real life.

We have an innovative culture, an environment that supports critical thinking and inventing. We also have an entrepreneurial culture, one that encourages people to turn those inventions into businesses.

We need both innovation and entrepreneurship. Both sustain a vibrant society, and both are critical to economic growth. We need innovators to dream up the impossible and entrepreneurs to make the dreams possible. And the impossible is happening more and more often.

One could argue that this culture of innovation and entrepreneurship itself helped usher in the New Normal, and that may very well be true.

What's absolutely certain is that the opportunities of the near future – in business, industry, finance, education, etc. – are as big or bigger than they've ever been.

If the U.S. continues to have a culture of leaders and entrepreneurs, if we seize decision superiority – if we see first, understand first and act first – the New Normal is ours.

But we have some significant challenges to overcome, and those challenges are part of our culture, too.

– Photos courtesy of the National Aeronautics and Space Administration (NASA)

Throughout U.S. history our people have demonstrated a culture of innovation and creativity and a willingness to take on the seemingly impossible. One of the most dramatic examples is the U.S. space program that placed men on the moon in the summer of 1969. That's Buzz Aldrin conducting a seismic experiment (above) and saluting the American Flag (left). Astronaut Neil Armstrong, commander of the lunar landing mission, took the pictures.

U.S. education system
in need of modernization

Our education system isn't adequately preparing our kids for the New Normal. We still have an education system geared to the industrial age and based on the agricultural cycle, as opposed to the information cycle. That nine months on and three months off calendar is bad for kids and bad for learning.

Kids with a whole lot of unsupervised time on their hands don't always turn it to good use – most juvenile crime occurs in July and August – and studies show that over the summer kids forget about a month's worth of what they learned in school.

We just can't have an educational system designed for the kids who went to school in the 19th century! It doesn't work. And you can tell it's not working because American kids are falling far behind students in numerous other countries. The 2009 Program for International Student Assessment test scores showed that American kids were twenty-third in the world in science scores, seventeenth in reading, and thirty-first in math.

Now, a lot of people think that American kids are doing so badly in school because the educational system is underfunded. I doubt it. We spend more per pupil than most other countries in the world. Shoveling more money at the schools isn't going to magically bring up test scores.

Others think that the scores are related to poverty-stricken schools bringing down the national average. It's true that poor kids tend to do worse in school than rich or middle-class kids. But when I was growing up in a family of 12, I thought we had it the hardest of anyone in the world. That's what I thought until I grew up and saw some of the rest of the world.

In comparison to a lot of folks, my family was doing well. We had something to eat every day, we could find jobs, and even though every now and then we'd need to sell a calf to pay off the electric bill, at least we had a calf to sell.

Meanwhile, in the 1960s South Koreans were measuring out dinner by the rice grain – but they were serious about the education of their children. Fifty years later, South Korea is still poor, but their kids are sixth in science, second in reading, and fourth in math on the international assessment. South Korea is poor and is out-pacing us anyway. So I don't think it's a simple lack of money that keeps kids from doing well in school.

A lot of folks believe kids would be better students if they had better teachers. The Center for Public Education released a study in 2005 that stated, among other things:

"Having an effective teacher consistently rises to the top as the most important factor in learning – more so than student ethnicity or family income, school attended, or class size."

But not even their rigorous research could pin-point exactly what makes a teacher effective or ineffective.

So what are we supposed to do for our children? My suggestion: Take a lot closer look at how they spend their time.

In all this talk about education, rarely do we get around to talking about the kids themselves. We know they're not learning enough math or science or reading. But they must be learning something – that's what kids' brains are wired to do. So what are they learning that prepares them for the New Normal?

Not much. What they see in the media is booty culture, gangster culture, TV shows that glorify rich idiots, and video games that predispose some kids to be killers.

Just as dangerous in the New Normal is the entitle-ment culture, which promotes the idea that everyone is entitled to what he or she wants. That we're all en-titled to a government-paid college education, a job, whatever we want – and someone else can pay for it.

That kind of thinking led to the global recession. The richest folks on Wall Street felt entitled to a few more millions, so they invented a new category of mortgages, picked the worst ones, got ratings agen-cies to label them Triple-A, and then sold these toxic assets to any sucker who would buy them, including their own customers.

The fallout from that greed-a-thon severely damaged the global economy. Yet the feeling of entitlement persists: The financial industry is pulling every string in Washington to keep consumer-centric regulation at bay.

That approach to things will not work in the New Normal. That kind of culture didn't even work before the whole world changed. But now – when we're so closely connected, the change cycle is so fast, and the opportunities are so big – it's a recipe for disaster.

Instead, we need a culture of see first, understand first and act first, and we need to start teaching it early in the education process. We need to produce citizens who can be innovators and entrepreneurs, who are trained from their earliest days to see, understand and act – and not just for their own selfish interests.

We need a *bona fide* culture change, not just talk. That culture change starts with the leaders of the New Normal.

The obvious need
for greater responsibility

You've no doubt seen the bumper sticker "Freedom Isn't Free." It was probably on a soldier's car. That message is popular with the military because it reminds them and civilians that great gain takes great sacrifice. Service people are proud to make that sacrifice.

But they shouldn't be the only ones sacrificing.

You will get out of life what you put into it. Whether you live to age 65 depends on what you're doing when you're 18, 25, 35 and 45. If we believe that we're entitled to bad diets, bad behavior, and bad ethics when we're young, we'll pay for it later. Freedom isn't free.

What we demand of ourselves now is what we live with later, for good or bad. Living well and long is a matter of personal responsibility. It's also a matter of decision superiority.

Consider the bridge that collapsed in Minneapolis in 2007. Six people died because the bridge wasn't fixed when it needed to be.

Or the infamous BP oil spill of 2010. The company was permitted to continue operating after 18 pollution citations, 16 fires and other accidents, and the evacuation of 77 workers when a platform started to sink. Then a pipe exploded, eleven people were killed, and we still don't know how many gallons of oil were released into the Gulf of Mexico or what the damage will be ultimately.

Then there are the New Orleans levees and seawalls that gave way to the power of Hurricane Katrina. More than 1,800 people died in Louisiana and Mississippi and 400,000 homes were lost as a result of that storm.

This is what comes of permitting chief financial officers more power than engineers and risk-management experts. You'll hear that lack of funding prevents us from doing risk containment. Hogwash! There's always money somewhere. If you close a bridge for just a week, the money to fix it is going to show up.

And it's dumb to assume that disaster will never strike and that precautionary measures are a waste. Bad things will always happen, and it costs a lot more to fix them than to prevent them. A lot more. Seeing first, understanding first, and acting first – being *responsible* – saves money, time and sometimes lives.

That's true for individuals, nations and businesses as well. Organizations are no more entitled to success or even survival than anyone else. Companies that refuse accountability or shift it off onto someone else are not taking decision superiority. They're reacting.

We're going to have to make sacrifices for the good of the country, and the first thing we're going to need to give up is our sense of entitlement. Whether it's increasing the taxes on the top 20 percent of U.S. citizens (who have 85 percent of the country's wealth) or discouraging lower-income folks from having out-of-wedlock babies – it's time for our people to step up.

A lot of us already have. There are citizens who return their Social Security funds to the government because they don't need them. Some have put solar panels on their roofs and greenhouses in their yards not only to save money but to save the environment. There are doctors who volunteer their time in free clinics and carpenters who build houses for Habitat for Humanity in their spare time.

Now, here's an interesting thing: People who do the right thing rarely are recognized and rewarded, and people who do the wrong thing rarely get punished.

Where's the outrage that none of the Wizards of Wall Street, whose greed crippled an economy, have gone to jail?

Why is no one horrified that the government sells flood insurance for houses on flood plains?

Why are teenage parents smiling from the covers of national entertainment magazines?

As a nation, we know better. We know that a government that lives in fear of TV talking heads is a weak government. We know that a little bit of moral judgment is good for a society because it keeps our worst impulses in check. We know that a selfish attitude – "I got mine, Jack, and to hell with you" – is bad for everyone. We have better morals, better standards and better principles than that.

Now, I am by no means calling for socialism. Like a lot of people who've spent time in socialist countries, I think socialism is a poor and limiting system. What I am talking about is accepting responsibility. Part of taking decision superiority is accepting the responsibility that goes with it. Our free market system is based on people doing what they say they're going to do. It is not based on making laws for the convenience of Goldman Sachs.

Of course, there are a lot of folks who say regulation prevents job growth and that the law pokes its nose into what is, or should be, a matter of business ethics. Everyone with good sense knows there isn't enough law to prevent people from doing stupid or unethical things. But when they do, they need to pay for it. That's one of the points of regulation – to hold violators accountable.

Free markets can't survive when no one is held accountable for what he or she does.

Political leaders must be keen enough to pick up on a cultural or economic shift and make good decisions – to see, understand and act first – for the common good. But they don't always recognize and take action on what they should. When they don't, we see things like the BP oil spill.

For example, years before the oil spill, the Minerals Management Service (MMS) of the Department of the Interior had a "dearth of regulations" and a "completely backwards" method of investigating spills and accidents, according to its own internal investigator.

But the MMS had a pretty clear approach to corruption, graft and sexual misconduct: They appeared to be all for it. *The New York Times* reported:

"Eight [MMS] officials . . . accepted gifts from energy companies whose value exceeded limits set by ethics rules – including golf, ski and paintball outings; meals and drinks; and tickets to a Toby Keith concert, a Houston Texans football game and a Colorado Rockies baseball game."

The Department of Interior's Inspector General filed a report with Congress that said several MMS officials "frequently consumed alcohol at industry functions, had used cocaine and marijuana, and had sexual relationships with oil and gas company representatives."

Can there be any wonder that no one at the MMS bothered to see if the oil rig was safe?

*   *   *

Does anyone honestly believe disaster will never happen again? It will. Another oil rig will explode, more bridges will collapse, other levees and seawalls will fail. And when they do, a lot of people will suffer.

A lot fewer will suffer, though, if we stop thinking someone else will bail us out. We shouldn't expect government, or any institution, to keep us safe. A lot of times they do, but sometimes they don't. We have to be prepared to be our own first responders.

In other words, followers must be accountable for their actions as well. If all the "baby daddies" in this country were held accountable, there would be a lot fewer kids growing up poor and fatherless. If Wall Street held itself accountable, it wouldn't confuse the word "sucker" with "customer."

The government is the obvious institution to hold these guys – or any other shameless, over-entitled crooks – accountable. But the government isn't in the mode to see first, understand first and act first. It is in the mode to react. That's the exact opposite of decision superiority.

It's not just political leaders, of course. Many social and business leaders have retreated into a risk-averse decision-making process, too. They're scared to death of criticism and in the case of political leaders, losing campaign funding, which amounts to the same thing. They've rejected decision superiority in favor of plausible deniability.

That's dangerous in the New Normal because so much of today's environment doesn't fit yesterday's ways of doing things. The New Normal is a comparatively abnormal situation, and in abnormal situations we have to use different ways of solving problems.

That's what people expect leaders to do. If leaders have the best of intentions, more often than not things turn out well. And even if they don't, the courage to make a decision can garner a lot of goodwill. President Theodore Roosevelt spoke highly of the virtues of decisiveness and right-thinking:

"In any moment of decision, the best thing you can do is the right thing. The worst thing you can do is nothing."

———— *Key points* ————

1. Criticism is something we can avoid easily by "saying nothing, doing nothing, and being nothing."
   – *Aristotle*

2. In the U.S. we have an innovative culture and environment that supports critical thinking and inventing.

3. Shoveling more money into the schools isn't going to magically bring up test scores.

4. We need to produce citizens who can be innovators and entrepreneurs.

5. Living well and long is a matter of personal responsibility.

6. We're going to have to make sacrifices for the good of the country, and the first thing we need to give up is our sense of entitlement.

Chapter 7

The true purpose of business

When bridges collapse, or airplane passengers spend the night on the runway, or an oil well explodes and causes unfathomable environmental damage, American business looks bad.

I mean it looks *really* bad – incompetent and shoddy, interested in cheaper and quicker rather than safer and better.

This assessment may seem like an unfair oversimplification, but it's how consumers feel.

I speak at seven or eight universities a year, and I have a standard question for business students:

"What is the purpose of business?"

Most say it's to make money. I tell them that's not the right answer, not in this day and age. I understand their point, of course, but it worries me that

119

our future business leaders would have such a simple, self-serving mindset.

Making money isn't good enough anymore. Only about 44 percent of new businesses survive to their fourth anniversary, and I attribute a lot of that to the failure of the quicker-and-cheaper paradigm.

If the purpose of your business is only to make money, your whole focus will be on turning a profit. You'll do whatever you have to do to make that profit. Whatever your product is, it will be made quickly and cheaply, not well, to minimize expenses in order to maximize profit.

In any case, Americans can't make anything cheapest or quickest these days. For one thing, there's always less costly labor somewhere else – first Mexico, then China, now Malaysia. And soon Malaysia will lose out to some other labor source.

Meanwhile, as I mentioned before, we are all inextricably linked in the New Normal. One hundred years ago, a mail-order company used to depend only on itself, its suppliers and the U.S. Postal Service. That's it.

Now, it depends on itself, its suppliers, the Post Office, FedEx, UPS, its website administrators, some server farm, an ad agency, the ad agency's freelancers, whomever it outsources the payroll to, the impact of the Middle East's political situation on the price of gas, and a dozen other things. We are tied to each other, for better or for worse. We're dependent on one another to the max.

That's why cheaper-and-quicker is the wrong model for business in the New Normal. It's not competitive, because anyone can get something cheaper somewhere else. It's not cost-effective, because when one little thing goes wrong anywhere along the supply chain, the whole operation gets screwed up and customers start defecting.

Many modern leaders have come to this same conclusion, and from there they have figured out the real purpose of business: to solve problems.

And with this realization comes a great opportunity for those who choose to take decision superiority – to see first, understand first and act first.

Find the right problem and solve it – and get rich in the process!

It's a lot smarter, and financially healthier, to sell what people *need* rather than what people *want*. Businesses that sell only what people want are very susceptible to economic and market downturns. Such companies have to be very nimble and resourceful to navigate those shifts in the marketplace. When money gets tight, what's the first thing people cut out of their budgets? The things they *want*, not the things they *need*.

And what people need is to have their problems solved. So, if you want to have a job, solve a problem. And the bigger the problem, the better.

Want to get rich?

Make an automobile that doesn't require any carbon-based energy. You'll solve a problem and you'll create a whole new industry, just like Bill Gates did.

Invent a machine that detects dirty bombs before they get on a plane.

Build a water platform that cleans water coming out of dairy farms.

Find a new or better way to feed the two billion people who will be born in the next few decades. You'll get rich, and you might avert a war.

Better yet, find a way to get fresh water where it's needed most. The world's next great wars will be fought over water, not oil. If we solve the problems associated with water, we can help prevent war in Africa, Asia and the Middle East. While the Israelis and the Palestinians argue about politics, at the heart of their problems is water, not religion. Most of the Middle East's problems for the past 3,000 years have had to do with access to water.

Now, oil presents some significant problems, too. The U.S.'s dependence on oil from the Middle East, and to a certain extent, South America, makes us very vulnerable. Most of the world's oil comes from countries with religious, political or social agendas that differ substantially from ours in the West. As long as we buy their oil, we fund their agendas. As we've seen, sometimes those agendas are pushed with guns or hijacked planes.

China is taking decision superiority in the chase for the energy of the future. China is doing more research on and putting more work into non-carbon, non-oil-based energies than anyone else in the world. But they're not applying it at home. For domestic use, they're just building more dumb, coal-based energy plants. China's research into New Normal energy is an investment focused strictly on the West.

And when they've got a lock on it, we'll pay through the nose. We'll have no choice, because 20th century energy will be too expensive in terms of blood and treasure for us to keep using it. That will be part of the New Normal of the future.

Treat your customers like patients on life-support!

The importance of customer care in the New Normal cannot be over-emphasized. Without customers, no business would exist. Retaining a solid base of faithful customers is a life-or-death matter for every business.

Attracting new customers – which can be done with well-targeted advertising and marketing – is one thing. Keeping those customers satisfied, short term and long term, is another matter altogether.

The most effective means I know to retain customers is to treat them like patients on life-support – as though their very survival depended on you. In other words, give them very close attention and take care of their needs as they relate to the goods or services sold by your company.

Top-flight customer care means your whole organization needs to listen closely to your customers. You have to do your homework. You have to know practically as much about your customers' business as they do.

This competitive advantage starts at the top of the organization. Leadership has to take decision superiority and communicate that *this* is how the company is going to run – that customers are to be thought of and treated as patients.

Once this policy is accepted and taken to heart by everyone who leads or works for the company, the organization must find ways to customize its service. For instance, nurses don't give every patient potassium shots just because potassium shots are on their carts. Nurses give people what they need individually. Translated, this means finding ways to make your goods or services fit each customer's particular needs.

For the culture of great customer service to become an integral part of your company's normal business operation, everyone in the organization must be onboard with it – owners, managers, salespeople, clerical and accounting staff, research and development people.

If everyone on your staff treats customers with great attention, care and expertise, your organization becomes the customers' partner – the kind of partner the customer can hardly live without.

And if your company is necessary to the continued survival of its customers, it has found the right problem to solve. It has found the true purpose of business.

Resiliency: The ability to come back after a sudden change

Even the most needed products, no matter what they are, won't secure a poorly led organization, or one in which the workforce can't cope with change.

After Hurricane Katrina, the only silver lining anyone could find was the great opportunity at hand for people in the construction and home-repair business.

But many of our small contractors lost their homes in the storm – and water washed away their businesses, too. They were the last in line to take advantage of the rebuilding boom because their tools were buried under a foot of toxic mud. Some were hired by out-of-town companies, but they couldn't profit from planning and directing the construction. They became construction laborers as opposed to contractors.

So, though a lot of local carpenters, plumbers and electricians had all the skills New Orleans needed, Hurricane Katrina crippled them. They had the skills, but they didn't have the resiliency to remain in business on their own.

Persistence

Nothing in the world can take the
place of persistence.
Talent will not; nothing is more
common than unsuccessful men
with talent.
Genius will not; unrewarded genius is
almost a proverb.
Education will not; the world is full of
educated derelicts.
Persistence and determination alone
are omnipotent.
The slogan "Press On!" has solved and
always will solve the problems of the
human race.

— Calvin Coolidge

That's not very unusual. Twenty-five percent of all businesses fail after a major natural disaster, and 40 percent of small businesses crash within five years of one.

But it doesn't take a catastrophe to kill off a business. Other things can be fatal, too: a CEO stepping down, market changes, new regulations.

More often than not, it's not an event that'll cause the destruction of a business, but the business's lack of resiliency that does it.

Resiliency is the ability to come back and be effective after a change – the ability to re-form a staff, to re-open a business, and to adjust.

The New Normal has brought some big changes. And, in my opinion, too few companies have the resiliency to cope with them.

Like a muscle, resiliency can be built up. And like muscle-building, the process is uncomfortable. It's natural to want to avoid pondering the worst that can happen. Most companies would rather put their resources into the actual challenges of the day, not the possible problems of the future. Some leaders simply can't imagine a natural disaster, or a serious downturn in the market, or they truly don't think these things will happen to them, so they don't bother with contingency plans.

Then the bridge collapses, or the levees fail, or the company's orders dry up suddenly, and no one knows what to do.

When trouble hits, an organization has to adjust immediately, and the leader's first job is to work through the chaos and confusion, not add to it. Establish priorities, because you can't do everything at once. Take the quick wins, do the simplest necessary tasks. These will inspire confidence and collaboration.

Leaders who can do this well can get their companies through a catastrophe. But, as we've seen, almost as many companies collapse in the aftermath of a disaster as fall apart as a direct result of it. I think this is because of lack of resiliency – and because they are forced into survival mode but never get out of it.

When the U.S. economy slowed in 2008-09, a lot of organizations "right-sized." That makes sense: Cut payroll, save money, keep the company solvent. That's called survival mode.

But growth does not come from survival mode; it comes from innovation. Growth comes from inventing and taking advantage of new technologies that give you the ability to perform as effectively and efficiently as possible. Growth comes from having a good product and selling it at the best value.

You can't remain in the survival mode indefinitely, because if you're not growing, you're falling behind.

And here's something else to consider: Not all game-changers are catastrophic. Good changes can hamstring organizations, too. Leaders need to recognize that it doesn't necessarily matter if the change is positive or negative. Big alterations of any kind usually require new responses, and that can throw a whole team off their game – unless they're resilient, unless leadership maintains a clear vision of the company's mission, short term and long term.

There's a story about a pig that illustrates this point.

The tale of the championship pig

Just when the global recession was getting to be its worst, I was in the boardroom of a big company, and the board members and the CEO were talking about selling one of their most valuable holdings.

"This little company right here is worth a good bit of money," they were saying. "If we sell it, we could pay off our debts and the money that we owe to our retirement fund."

"Whoa, wait a minute!" I said. "Let me tell you a story about my pig."

I tell you, offer to tell a story about a pig to a room of anxious executives, and you'll get some attention.

So I told them my story. When I was a senior in high school my dad and I went out to a pig breeder's lot to buy a pig for my 4-H project. I got the pick of the litter, a boar hog, for about $18. He was just a baby coming off his mother. We put him in the back of the truck and took him home, and I raised him like a pet. He was a great pig. Man, I loved that pig! And I won the 4-H State Championship with him.

When we came back from the state fair, word was out in our area that my pig was a champion. The next day a farmer stopped by and asked to talk to my dad. He told dad he'd buy that pig for $125. (At the time, you could have bought the best pig in the world for $100.) So I had a dilemma. What do I do? Do I sell the pig or keep him for stud?

It was a tough choice. I was going to be starting college in a few months, the first in my family of 12 children to do so. I needed that $125 in the worst way, but I knew that if my pig was performing stud services at different farms all the time, I'd have a little money coming in every week. Better yet, we'd get the pick of the litters that my pig would sire.

So I kept that bad boy and for about two years he had a grand life, until he got too big and too ornery to move around very well. Even then people would bring their sows to him. We still got one piglet from every litter.

When I finished that story, we discussed the company's options.

"I think you're considering selling a state champion pig right now," I said.

I asked them, Do we want short-term gain or do we want to grow the business? Do we want to figure out how we can get out of this survival mode and go into growth mode? My old pig was a producer, and so is the little company you're thinking of selling, I reasoned.

The board bought my line of thinking and agreed to hang on to their little company, opting for long-term growth. They kept their championship pig, as it were.

*   *   *

How you bounce back from a change, especially a big one, matters. A lot of leaders think holding a company together is sufficient, but it's not. Even when the water is up to their knees, leaders need to be thinking of growing, not just getting by.

That's hard. Believe me, I've been in water up to my knees, literally. But that's why organizations have leaders.

When times are easy and there aren't any bad choices, leaders can coast. But in times of trouble, everyone depends on the folks in charge. They don't care if leadership is worried or confused or tired. They just want to know what the plan is.

And I can say this with certainty: Plans crafted toward growth and solving customers' problems are the ones most likely to see organizations through troubled waters.

— *Key points* —

1. Cheaper, better and quicker nearly destroyed the American automobile industry.

2. New Normal leaders understand that the purpose of business is to solve people's problems.

3. Find a new or better way to feed the two billion people who will be born in the next few decades, and you'll get rich and might even prevent a war.

4. The world's next great wars will be fought over water, not oil.

5. Treat your customers like patients on life-support, and they'll be yours for a long, long time.

6. Twenty-five percent of all businesses fail after major natural disasters, and 40 percent of small businesses crash within five years of them.

Chapter 8

Earning your subordinates' loyalty and investing in their success

Earlier on, I stated my working definition of leadership: the art and science of influencing others to willingly follow. To accomplish this, to get willing followers, leaders need to do two things: they must walk the walk and they must inspire loyalty.

Leaders have to be genuinely respectable. They need to live up to the best attributes of the organizations they lead. Good leaders are good citizens. Followers want somebody who's respectable, not just somebody who's loud.

I learned in the military that people follow, or appear to be following, because of the perceived power of the leader, not necessarily because of the ideas the leader professes. Now, in the military, followers *have* to obey, whether they want to or not. There are all kinds of penalties for people who don't obey, such as discharge or court-martial.

But no one, in uniform or not, has to obey willingly. And people who obey unwillingly are bad followers. Oh, they'll do what they're told – but not one thing more – and they'll do it as badly as they can get away with.

Good followers, however, obey *willingly* because the mission is as important to them as it is to the leader. They'll do their jobs well to the point of excellence, do it fast and efficiently, and they'll make the leader look like a genius.

The Gallup Organization has done a lot of research into inspired followers – what they call "engaged workers" – and found that these workers are much more productive and profitable, get hurt less, are more loyal, and somehow create willing customers. Engaged workers achieve all that only if they have good leadership.

And good leadership has something to do with presence. A leader's presence isn't just a matter of power, or decision-making authority, or control over resources. A real leader isn't even elected; some elected officials think they're leaders when, in fact, they're just figureheads. Their constituencies aren't following, they're just waiting out the election cycle.

I'm not entirely sure that even the best leaders can truly lead on a national scale. It's possible the country is simply too fractured for that. It's a certainty that a number of people make a lot of money keeping it that way. It hasn't always been like that, however.

After the Revolutionary War, George Washington was practically worshipped in America. Some people wanted to create a new American monarchy with him as King; others wanted Washington to accept a lifetime presidency. He refused all that, but nevertheless he became an icon. Think of how many places and things are named for him – Washington, D.C., Washington State, the Washington monument, bridge, college and arch. Even today, the dollar you stick in a vending machine has his picture on it.

Washington inspired that kind of response not because he won a war, but because he won his followers. Americans saw him as a real leader, the person to speak for them in their absence, to put their best interests ahead of his own, a man who saw the future and led them to it.

Leaders must say what they mean and mean what they say. Followers don't score you on where you come from or necessarily what you look like. They score you on your character. As soldiers like to say, your audio and your video have to match.

This is not to say that followers require a leader who is perfect. In fact, I think followers recognize that leaders are *necessarily* imperfect. After all, leadership is a human endeavor, and humans are flawed creatures. Pretend to have no flaws, and you'll lose your credibility. Accept your flaws – and demonstrate that you're working on them – and you'll inspire some trust. And if you inspire enough trust, you'll attract loyalty.

Leadership and Integrity

In order to be a leader a man must have followers. And to have followers a man must have their confidence. Hence, the supreme quality for a leader is unquestionably integrity. Without it, no real success is possible, no matter whether it is on a section gang, a football field, in an army, or in an office. If a man's associates find him guilty of being phony, if they find that he lacks forthright integrity, he will fail. His teachings and actions must square with each other. The first great need, therefore, is integrity and high purpose.

– Dwight D. Eisenhower

Loyalty and obedience
are two different things

Loyalty is largely based on emotion but manifests itself in action.

If we feel that a leader is on the right track, we'll follow him or her. Retired Army General Colin Powell once said that loyal followers will follow their leader if for no other reason than simple curiosity.

But sometimes leaders don't understand that while loyalty and obedience look alike, they are two different things. Leaders will experience significant problems if they don't know the difference between the two. It's possible for people to be close to their leader, and still not be loyal. The worst that can come from a bunch of disloyal followers is total mission failure. More common is slow mission malfunction. It's hard to blame that on any one person, but it can be the result of disloyalty.

Slow malfunctions in mission occur when disloyal followers report things to their leader in a certain way – a way that's good for the follower but may be bad for the mission. Or followers will report some things to leadership and other things to their fellow followers.

When that happens, the rumor mill is much more powerful than the chain of command. Sometimes things are left undone; other times things are done but done badly. When the malfunction is discovered, the followers responsible tend to put all their energy into covering their back-sides rather than fixing the problem.

At the end of the day, the mission is what matters, more than the leader or the followers. What the organization is trying to accomplish should be central to everyone's sense of loyalty.

History shows that loyalty to leaders and not organizations can, in its worst forms, come to demagoguery. Loyalty to leaders is good, but loyalty to leaders *and* the organization is better.

How to pick your followers? Very carefully!

In many organizations, leaders don't get to choose their followers. Often, they inherit them. But just about everybody gets to pick the people closest to them, their executive team. As time goes by, leaders can choose replacements for the team members who leave. When that happens, it pays to pick your closest followers very carefully.

Choosing subordinates is one of the most important decisions a leader can make. We think of leaders as the brains of the operation, the people who make decisions, create strategies, maintain control, and determine the fate of an organization. It's true, they do. But all the activities that result from those decisions are carried out by subordinates.

The mission of an organization is rarely implemented in detail by the leader. It's almost always carried out, day by day and minute by minute, by followers. Leaders of large businesses usually don't interact directly with customers or the public; subordinates do.

Weak leaders tend to pick the worst subordinates. Often, they'll eliminate any subordinate who appears to be a threat. The mere fact of feeling threatened is a sign of weak leadership. And weak leaders are always threatened by subordinates who are smarter than they are.

Strong leaders, on the other hand, look for followers who are smarter and more capable than they are themselves – especially in areas where the leaders may be lacking. There's wisdom in this approach in that it makes for a more well-rounded team. For instance, if you use a lot of numbers in your work but aren't good at math, you should have someone around who is. This improves the organization's chances for overall mission success.

To fulfill the mission now and grow the organization over the long term, leaders obviously have to pick the best subordinates they can. This is an essential part of decision superiority: picking people for their potential and ability and not for their personality. Remember, the New Normal is going to throw things at you that you can't even imagine right now, so you need people around you who can cope with change.

Selecting followers for their potential and competence pretty well guarantees a variety of personality types, and not necessarily harmonious ones. Sometimes leaders shy away from that, thinking that hiring a bunch of people who are so different creates the potential for a riot.

That may be so, but remember, good leaders inspire loyalty to themselves and the organization. They take decision superiority, and they make sure their people don't have mere jobs but missions. These virtues inspire confidence and pull a team together even when personality conflicts could have torn it apart. Ultimately, good leaders and good, clear missions are stronger than the forces of chaos.

Besides those who are smarter than you, there are certain kinds of other people you should have on your team, including unambitious bureaucrats and bothersome contrarians.

One very common mistake is to reject people who seem totally disinterested in having a leadership position. These include bureaucrats, office workers. Folks like these just come to work. They want to be left alone; they're not interested in being a hotshot. They want to come to their desks, do their jobs, and then go home.

That doesn't make them unwilling or disloyal. It just means they're not ambitious. But if they're good at their jobs, they are worth their weight in gold because they get routine, necessary things done.

Good bureaucrats – and every organization needs

them – get the forms filed, keep you conformed to safety laws, know where everything is kept, abide by the tax codes, respond to customers promptly, and on and on. Just by nature of their personalities, they help keep organizations from going off the rails. They aren't going to set the world on fire with outstanding achievement, but they're essential. Don't take them for granted.

Another vital group is folks I call contrarians. While a lot of leaders are uncomfortable with contrarians, I think they can be good for an organization.

Contrarians keep leaders from accepting "groupthink." Leaders tend to avoid contrarians because they seem to inspire dissension, cause problems, maybe slow things down. And, to be honest, sometimes leaders just don't feel like being challenged by subordinates.

Contrarians don't just nod at everything you say; they point out what's wrong with what you just said. That's a vital function because it can prevent mistakes, sometimes very serious ones. I think every organization needs somebody playing that role; a lot of organizations find it in their lawyers and their CFOs. Your organization is a lot more likely to base strategy on reality rather than ideology if you're lucky enough to have a CFO or lawyer who stops you in your tracks and makes you look at things from a legal viewpoint or a stockholder's perspective.

But here is one of the real benefits of picking

good followers: They contribute to the success of the mission by picking good subordinates themselves. In most well-run organizations, the mission starts at the top and trickles down. If subordinates are poorly chosen, the mission will get bottlenecked at the top and never flow smoothly from there.

In a big organization, a lot can get lost along the way in the chain of command. Subordinates chosen for the right reasons – for their potential and ability rather than their personality – are more likely to choose people under them who are capable of upholding the mission all along the chain.

Once the right team is selected, leaders need to keep its members growing and developing. Leaders do that by investing in subordinates' success.

The right training: A key investment in the mission

The first and most obvious method of investing in subordinates' success is ongoing training. The military is excellent at this. We keep our folks in a constant state of training. A good soldier can get trained to do anything he or she wants if the right aptitude is demonstrated.

Schooling is great for organizations. New information, new materials, new thinking, new ways of doing things bring efficiency, productivity and excitement.

Remember the American automotive industry in the early 1980s? For decades the Big Three U.S.

automakers ignored Japanese manufacturing methods. Then Toyota, Honda and others took a huge percentage of the customers away. Suddenly, Detroit was desperate to learn what Toyota already knew.

Almost immediately, all the U.S. car execs were talking about *kaizen* (on-going improvement) and were totally immersed in lean manufacturing, process improvement, waste elimination, just-in-time delivery, order-based production and market-based pricing. Cars got a lot better as a result – safer, better-built and less costly to manufacture and run.

Training is also great for the mission. People who are brimming with knowledge bring some vitality with them to the workplace. That vitality is like a booster shot for the mission. The most willing followers are the most excited ones, and if the training excites the worker, his or her identification with the mission will get a boost, too.

It's important, therefore, to pick the right training, for two reasons.

First, the right training will teach your followers how to do their jobs better. The wrong training will be a waste of their time and your budget.

Second, the right training will show that you're paying attention, that you care. The right training is tailored to the worker, and if the leader knows exactly what the right training is and cares enough to invest in the worker, the worker will feel known and cared for as an individual. That's an essential part of worker engagement, according to Gallup research.

So what is the right training? That depends, since each situation is different. Of course, all workers need to learn about the laws that apply to their work. All employees need to be trained on relevant safety issues. But other than that, training is an individual thing.

In addition to the more concrete forms of training – in sales, marketing, graphic arts techniques, firing a weapon, building a house, etc. – there are numerous more abstract forms, such as leadership training.

In the Army, if you show leadership qualities, we'll give you ample opportunities to expand on them. Civilian workers also have myriad leadership training programs, some better and more useful than others.

When you send an employee to such training, especially a frontline worker, you'll be rewarded above and beyond what the program provides. There is nothing more flattering or meaningful – nothing more engaging – than being told you show leadership potential.

Some organizations offer tuition reimbursement – they cover some or all of the costs of college for their employees. I've seen this work very well, and I've seen it backfire: You pay for someone's PhD, and they take it to a competitor who offers better pay. A lot of companies try to prevent this by stipulating that the new graduate can't quit for some period of time. But do you really want a worker who's counting the minutes until he or she can resign? There's nothing *willing* in a worker like that, nothing customer- or mission-oriented.

So I think that if the organization is going to put someone through college, it should be an employee who has already demonstrated genuine devotion and loyalty to the company. This is another form of the right training of the right person – all to the benefit of mission success.

Embracing technology:
A prerequisite to success

Another way to invest in your subordinates' success is to embrace technology. This can be hard for some leaders to do.

Most of us are completely comfortable with the technology we knew in our youth. Does the telephone intimidate you? Of course not. Does e-mail seem difficult to operate? Probably not. Can you network your smart phone through your company's servers and back through your home printer while constructing and/or evading all the necessary firewalls along the way? If you can, you're probably under the age of 40.

High school students are totally comfortable with and have access to better technology than NASA did when they launched the first Apollo flights. By the time today's toddlers are in college, they'll have and be totally comfortable with technology that we can't even imagine.

I remember when the Army started putting computers on every desk – man, some people came close to mutiny. But they learned how to use the computer and stopped glaring at it all day. This kind of thing happened in organizations all over the world, and it probably will continue to as long as technology evolves (forever, in other words).

Then, there are those who are enthused about every new technology that comes along. They were the first to know what an "app" is and what to do with it, the kind who have more gadgets in their junk drawer than most people have in their house. They think of technology as interesting and fun – but, more importantly, they know it helps get the work done.

Getting the work done efficiently advances the mission. So I recommend embracing technology and giving your subordinates the equipment they need.

You'll get flak from your techno-phobes. Just tell them you realize there's a learning curve to technology, but that the curve starts steeply and drops off quickly. You may need to hold some hands at first, but workers never reject a thing once they realize it makes their jobs easier and their lives better.

Tech lovers, however, need to recognize that not everything that beeps is useful. I suggest you deal with these folks by having them carefully research the technology they want. Then buy it if they can convince you it will advance the mission.

Technology is an aid to decision superiority, in that it helps us to see first, understand first and act first. This principle is clearly illustrated in the war in Afghanistan, in which the U.S. is using unmanned drones (above) to locate and kill the enemy, while Taliban soldiers (below) are fighting a guerilla war using weapons with little or no technological sophistication.

By now, it should be abundantly clear that the efficient use of technology contributes to decision superiority. It helps leaders and followers to see first, understand first and act first.

The war in Afghanistan illustrates this point. The Taliban is fighting a guerilla war because they don't have the technology to do anything else. They didn't invest in it. The American military is countering the Taliban with drones and high-resolution satellite video.

Granted, most of our knowledge of the Taliban's plans comes from human intelligence – that's how we found out where Osama bin Laden was holed up – but we're conducting a good bit of our warfare technologically. So while the Taliban is burning through its recruits, we're preventing the deaths of thousands of our service people and non-combatants and taking out the enemy through the careful application of technologically guided weapons.

Technology works the same way in the business world. If you know the lay of the land in every detail – inventory, the competition, marketing, distribution, manufacturing in all its layers – you can make better decisions. There's almost no way of doing that anymore without some pretty sophisticated technology. If you have it and understand it, you can make better decisions. You can see first, understand first, and act first.

Another way to say this is that technology is a

telescope into the future, a set of tools that helps us plan and implement winning strategies.

Remember, solving problems is the purpose of business, and the right technology helps to solve problems. So, give your subordinates the technology they need and the training to understand it and you'll not only be investing in their success, but in your organization's success as well.

——— *Key points* ———

1. Good followers obey willingly because the mission is as important to them as it is to their leaders.

2. Followers don't judge their leaders on where they come from or necessarily what they look like. They score leaders on character and presence.

3. Loyalty is based largely on emotion, but it manifests itself in action.

4. Choosing their principal subordinates is one of the most important decisions leaders make.

Chapter 9

Save your best leadership for when you get home

P eople who are very successful in their careers are almost always driven individuals. And this certainly applies to leaders. They've got something extra that drives them.

But they can be driven to the extent that their job becomes their world. Some of these guys prove the point that it is possible to win the world and lose your soul – and your family.

It's not hard to convince yourself that what you're doing is for the sake of your family. That all those hours and all that energy at work pays the tuition, creates status in the community, and is ultimately for the benefit of the people you love.

That's the common line of thought: You work hard, you achieve; you achieve, you get paid more;

you get paid more, you can afford quality schools, safe family cars, a decent house in a nice neighborhood, and everything else a family needs.

Be careful, however, that you don't spend so much time and energy providing for your family that you lose your family. If you don't have time to talk to your kids now, you'll wake up one day and see a bunch of strangers in your house. The kid who used to jump on your lap when you got home from work, the kid you couldn't shake off your leg if you wanted to, will walk in wearing nothing but black with pieces of metal sticking out all over her body. And when you ask her what happened at school today, she'll say, "Nothing."

What'd you do after school today?

"Not much."

You'd be lucky to get a four-word answer out of her.

You can win the world and lose your family. And they don't always come back.

Corporate leaders, military leaders, social leaders, government leaders, and every family breadwinner – they're all decisively engaged. They have to be. By the time you arrive at a leadership position, you'll have a track record of long hours, endurance, skill, wisdom and authority. To win at work takes energy, and there's only so much of that to go around.

So when you come home and see your kid who used to be a sweet, gentle child but is now somebody you hardly recognize, you may ask, "What the hell happened?" I'll tell you what happened: Your energy went elsewhere a long time ago. And now it may be too late.

The guidance, care and attention a family needs starts the day you bring a baby home. So does your leadership in the household.

A family is a team, and teams need leaders

As I stated earlier, leadership is the art of influencing people to willingly follow you to accomplish a task or a mission.

A family has a mission, too: to work as a team. And just like a team in the business world, members have to follow willingly or they aren't a team. They're a group. Groups will do what they're told if they're scared to disobey. But they won't accomplish much.

The fact is, families have a lot to accomplish and the New Normal makes it harder to do. Job competition is fiercer, none of us are as financially secure as we used to be, communities are fractured, and our value system is overly influenced by greed, glamour and entitlement.

In the midst of all this, families have to educate and support their young; create a healthy, stable, nurturing environment; and produce resilient, capable adults who can become good citizens and make successful lives of their own.

Meanwhile, families need to get to school on time, enroll kids in baseball, get homework assignments completed, decorate for the holidays, get everyone a flu shot, learn how to ride a bike and set a table, and remember to say "Thank you." To accomplish any of this, a family has to work as a team.

And teams need leading.

Parents are leaders; that's their role in the family. Now, too often what we find in the corporate world is that people may have no problem executing a leadership role at work, but they fail to execute their role as a leader at home. Either they don't pick up the baton or they use it as a club.

Families need leading because kids need teaching. As I mentioned earlier, a big part of leadership is teaching. Now, you can teach your kids by threat: "If you don't do this, I'm going to take your car, I'm going to restrict your movements, I'm going to take your phone."

But that's not leading. It doesn't create willingness to follow. It creates willingness to not get caught. When your child doesn't care about getting in trouble anymore, your authority is over.

If you don't lead your family, someone else will.

Don't let it get to that point. Lead your family. But don't think, not even for a minute, that what works at the office will work at home.

Exercising positive, collaborative leadership

If you're a leader at work, you've got control. You're the one who gives the orders.

"Hey, this report is full of errors and it's not supported by documentation. Go fix it," you might say.

And someone will fix it.

But there's no such function of command in the house. You can't say to your spouse:

"The food is not spiced correctly; my shirts are folded wrong. Go fix it."

You can't talk like that if you want to continue living there!

Leave your command hat at the door. You cannot use that style of leadership with a seven-year-old either. It won't work. And if you use that style of leadership with an adult, expect to be living alone very soon. When you walk in your front door, you're not in command; you're in collaboration.

It's easier to move a rope by pulling than it is by pushing. That's an aspect of positive, rather than negative, leadership. Negative leadership uses bossing and fear tactics: "If you don't tie your shoes I'm going to spank you; if you don't pull up your algebra grade you'll be grounded."

Positive leadership uses encouragement and goal-setting: "If you tie your shoes, we can go on a walk; I'll help you with your algebra homework so you can get your grades up."

* * *

One of the Army's principles of leading the troops is supervision of the accomplishment of the task. There isn't much the Army doesn't know about how to get a lot of people to accomplish a task efficiently and successfully. In fact, this eight-step process is followed by everybody from the top generals on down in the Army.

1. Receive the task or the mission.
2. Give a warning order with a date and time of when the task has to be performed.
3. Make a tentative plan.
4. Make necessary improvements. In other words, if you have to move to another location to perform this task, move.
5. Reconnaissance. Take a look at the terrain and see what kind of shape it's in and what else has to be done.
6. Complete the plan.
7. Issue a complete order. You gave the warning order, now make sure it's understood.
8. Supervise the execution of the task.

In this case, what we use in the Army can be used appropriately at home. So you don't just tell a kid, "Hey, go clean your room." Instead, you say:

"Okay, clean your room before lunch. Ask your mom where she keeps the duster. If you need help moving the bed, let me know. I'll be up in the next half hour to check."

And then, of course, you check.

* * *

When I was in the Army, I could always tell which commanders had kids and which didn't. The ones who didn't have kids had no tolerance for people not following the rules, very little patience for things not being done properly. Whereas people with kids know darn well that there's a little bit of kid still in all of us, and that it's wise to use what we call "verifiable trust." Or, as President Ronald Reagan liked to say, "Trust but verify."

Verifiable trust means trusting that the person will do what you say in a timely manner, and trusting that he knows you'll check.

When I told my daughter Stefanie to clean her room, she knew she had a task to do and that I trusted her to do it – and that I'd be checking later to make sure she did it according to the standard.

The challenge is making the standards clear. Does "clean your room" mean "take all your dirty clothes, footballs, old socks, and math book, and stuff them in the closet?"

The same principle applies in the workplace. You can be sure that if the standard is not clear, people will pick their own standard. And every time you ignore a mistake, you've just set a new standard.

158 *Leadership in the New Normal*

Inspire trust by
being trustworthy

The beauty of collaboration, of positive leadership, is that it makes followers more willing to follow and it inspires trust. You can inspire trust only by being trustworthy. You have to walk the walk. You can't tell your kids not to smoke, then go out to the patio and puff on a cigarette. You can't talk to your kids with any credibility about not using alcohol and drugs if they see you passed out on the couch. It's not your right as an adult to be abusive in language or behavior, and if you are you should expect your kids to demonstrate that behavior with their friends, siblings and peers.

If you want your kids to be trustworthy, you have to be trustworthy. And for your family to trust you, your audio and your video have to match, as we say in the Army.

And you *do* need them to trust you. Sooner or later something awful is going to happen and, as with all crises, the sooner you know about it the easier it is to fix.

Kids have questionable judgment. Sometimes they have terrible judgment. And in instances of terrible judgment, kids would rather tell you what you want to hear as opposed to what you need to hear. Because they're kids. (Actually, this is true of subordinates in general – but the good ones come clean!)

Communicate frequently enough and you can

sense that the answer you got is not necessarily the one you want to hear, but the truth. You'll develop that sense only after long engagement with the child. But kids are more likely to give you the truth immediately if they trust you.

Over the years I've learned a way of teaching people how to announce bad news. It's simple and straightforward: Just give them the bad news. Don't hide it. When something bad happens, or when discipline has been broken, or there's a disappointment in store, say so.

If you're not prepared to give bad news, then you'll never hear bad news directly from your kid. You'll hear it from a teacher or you'll hear it from a neighbor or you'll hear it from a cop. One way or another you'll hear it and it'll arrive in a most unpleasant way. If your kids don't think they can tell you bad news, they'll hide it from you.

Everybody with a long career of any kind has heard a lot of bad news. Handling it well is a matter of perspective. At work, we learn to deal with setbacks because, for one thing, they're inevitable, and for another, you can't fire everybody who screws up. Leadership is figuring out what went wrong, teaching subordinates to avoid making that mistake again, and returning to the pursuit of the mission at hand. There are few mistakes so bad that we can't recover from them.

So does a fender-bender mean you take away the

car? Does a baseball through a window pane result in being banned from the yard? No. It means another discussion about safe driving, another talk about being careful with baseballs.

As long as your kid is still alive and standing there talking to you, whatever happened wasn't that bad. As long as they know you feel that way, kids will communicate with you. As long as you can communicate, you can lead.

But don't forget, kids have to be taught that actions have consequences. No one is born knowing that.

Your kids will believe you only if they trust you. They'll trust you only if you earn that trust, day after day in the smallest ways you can imagine. They'll trust you if you always show up at the game when you say you will. They'll trust you if they ask for a turkey sandwich in their lunch box and you remember to fix it. They'll trust you if when you lose your temper you cool down fast – and you don't lose your temper often.

Mutual trust inspires loyalty to the family team; and loyalty to one another is an essential part of what it means to be a family.

The Warrior Ethos
works in families, too

There's a saying in the Army that all the troops know by heart: *I will always place the mission first. I will never accept defeat. I will never quit. I will never leave a fallen comrade.*

We call that the Warrior Ethos.

There's a parallel to this in the corporate world and at home. In each case, the central, guiding question should be the same: What is our mission?

The mission of parents should be to build a family team. So families should have an ethos as well.

Placing the mission first means *my family is more important to me than anything else.*

Never accepting defeat means *I won't give up trying. You may not like what I'm doing here, but I will not stop trying.*

Never quitting means *I'll be beside you, no matter how long it takes you to become the person you're meant to be.*

Never leaving a fallen comrade means *regardless of what you do, I will always love you. I will come to get you.*

I've thought about this a long time, how the Warrior Ethos works in families.

I've gotten letters from Military Police telling me they were called out to a colonel's house because there was a domestic disturbance, that my colonel was beating up on his kid.

What do you do with something like that? What do you do the next day when you're told that's one of the best colonels on the base?

Well, he might be the best colonel we have at work, but the best colonels I know don't have police coming to their house to put a stop to child abuse. Being successful at work is not the only indicator of success.

If you fail in parenting, what you do at work doesn't matter so much. But if you succeed in your mission of building a family team, you succeed at the most important responsibility you have.

* * *

I've said it before and I'll say again: Leadership is a calling, and a noble one. Leaders are vital to the ongoing success of our country, our society and our economy. Without leaders, we're all sled dogs running off a cliff.

But save your best leadership for when you get home. At the end of the day, kids need to know you care about them. When the family team is not formed, kids can't see that you care about them. They perceive they're a burden, not a blessing.

I was a soldier for 37 years, three months, and three days. I had a hell of a career. I learned more, became more, experienced more than I ever could have imagined. I worked with Presidents and the top brass of the military. I traveled all over the world, met some of the greatest leaders of our time, and saw things I'll never forget. I had a lot of fun and I hope I did some good in this world.

But on February 28, 2008, when I clocked out on my last day as a working Lieutenant General in the

U.S. Army and pulled up to my house, the President, the Joint Chiefs of Staff, and the thousands of troops I commanded were not there. My wife, Beverly, and our four children were the ones waiting for me to come home. My team.

Key points

1. Be careful not to spend so much time and energy providing for your family that you lose your family.

2. Leading at work is easy compared to leading at home.

3. A family has a mission: to work as a team. Families need leading because kids need teaching. A parent's proper role is to lead, to teach and to build a strong family unit.

4. Parents should remember: When you walk in your front door, you're not in command but in collaboration.

5. Parents shouldn't try to lead their families like officers commanding their troops; however, The Warrior Ethos used in the military works well to build a strong family team.

Sources

Books, magazine articles, and other printed documents

Bush, George W. *Decision Points*. New York: Crown Publishers, 2010.

Deaton, Angus, interview by Jennifer Robison. "News Flash: Money Does Buy Happiness." *Gallup Business Journal*, Jan. 2008.

Foundations of Leadership. BOLC I: Army ROTC Custom Edition. Boston: Pearson Custom Publishing, 2006.

Frame, Adela, and James W. Lussier. *66 Stories of Battle Command*. Fort Leavenworth, Kansas: U.S. Army Command and General Staff College Press, 2000.

Gallup, Alec M., and Frank Newport. *The Gallup Poll: Public Opinion 2006*. Lanham, Maryland: Rowman & Littlefield Publishers, 2007.

Gediman, Dan, John Gregory, and Mary Jo Gediman. *This I Believe: On Fatherhood*. San Francisco: Jossey-Bass, 2011.

Honoré, Lt. Gen. Russel L. (U.S. Army, Ret.) with Ron Martz. *Survival: How a Culture of Preparedness Can Save You and Your Family From Disasters*. New York: Atria Books, 2009.

Kaltman, Al. *Cigars, Whiskey, and Winning: Leadership Lessons from Ulysses S. Grant*. Special Armed Forces Edition. Paramus, New Jersey: Prentice Hall Press, 1998.

McCullough, David. *John Adams.* New York: Simon & Schuster Paperbacks, 2001.

McCullough, David. *1776.* New York: Simon & Schuster, 2005.

"The Nature and Extent of Delinquency." In *Juvenile Delinquency: Theory, Practice, and Law,* by Larry J. Siegel and Brandon C. Welsh, pp. 34-66. Belmont, California: Wadsworth Cengage Learning, 2009.

Newman, Maj. Gen. Aubrey "Red" (Ret.). *Follow Me: The Human Element in Leadership.* Novato, California: Presidio Press, 1981.

Nye, Roger H. *The Challenge of Command: Reading for Military Excellence.* Wayne, New Jersey: Avery Publishing Group, 1986.

O'Neil, William J., editor. *Military and Political Leaders and Success: 55 Top Military and Political Leaders and How They Achieved Greatness.* New York: McGraw-Hill, 2005.

Platt, Derrick E. "Language: Critical Components in Readers with Criminal Referral History." *Journal of Correctional Education* (Ashland University) Vol. 60, No. 4 (December 2009), pp. 277-288.

Richter, Frank-Jürgen, Faisal Hoque, and Mark Minevich. *Six Billion Minds.* Boston: Aspatore Inc., 2006.

Rowitz, Louis. *Public Health for the 21st Century: The Prepared Leader.* Sudbury, Massachusetts: Jones and Bartlett Publishers, 2006.

Warren, Rick. *The Purpose Driven Life: What On Earth Am I Here For?* Grand Rapids, Michigan: Zondervan, 2002.

Online

"AIDS Timeline." *AVERT.org.* http://www.avert.org/aids-timeline.htm.

Bjerga, Alan. "Food Stamp Recipients at Record 41.8 Million Americans in July, U.S. Says." *Bloomberg.* October 5, 2010. http://www.bloomberg.com/news/2010-10-05/food-stamp-recipients-at-record-41-8-million-americans-in-july-u-s-says.html.

Campbell, Anita. "Business Failure Rates Highest in First Two Years." *Small Business Trends.* July 7, 2005. http://smallbiztrends.com/2005/07/business-failure-rates-highest-in.html.

Clayton, Mark. "BP oil spill: MMS shortcomings include 'dearth of regulations.'" *The Christian Science Monitor.* June 17, 2010. http://www.csmonitor.com/USA/Politics/2010/0617/BP-oil-spill-MMS-shortcomings-include-dearth-of-regulations.

"Cradle to Prison Pipeline Campaign." *Children's Defense Fund.* 2012. http://www.childrensdefense.org/programs-campaigns/cradle-to-prison-pipeline/index.html.

Death Penalty Information Center. "Costs of Death Penalty." *DeathPenaltyInfo.org.* 2012. http://www.deathpenaltyinfo.org/costs-death-penalty.

Dunn, Andrew. "New regulations could reduce mosquito abatement programs." *StarNewsOnline.com.* March 17, 2011.http://www.starnewsonline.com/article/20110317/ARTICLES/110319675.

"Education." *Globalization101.* State University of New York Levin Institute. http://www.globalization101.org/education-2/.

Free Resources. "Country Profile and Demographics: Per Capita Income." *Free Resources Website.* April 16,

2009. http://siakhenn.tripod.com/capita.html.

"Ghana: Nation at 55 – Poised for a Great Leap Forward?" *allAfrica*. March 9, 2012. http://allafrica.com/stories/201203091485.html.

Gregory, Sean. "Cory Booker: The Mayor of Twitter and Blizzard Superhero." *TIME.com*. December 29, 2010. http://www.time.com/time/nation/article/0,8599,2039945,00.html.

"Haiti." *The New York Times*. August 16, 2012. http://topics.nytimes.com/top/news/international/countriesandterritories/haiti/index.html.

"History of Windows: Highlights from the first 25 years." *Microsoft Windows*. http://windows.microsoft.com/en-US/windows/history.

"Korea Average Salary Income - Job Comparison." *WorldSalaries.org*. 2005. http://www.worldsalaries.org/korea.shtml.

Kurpis, Brian. *Hurricane Katrina Relief*. http://www.hurricanekatrinarelief.com/.

Levitt, Theodore. "Marketing Myopia." *Harvard Business Review*. www.hbr.org, July-august, 2004. http://hbr.org/2004/07/marketing-myopia/ar/1?referral=00269.

Lindbergh Foundation and the Hall Aviation Foundation. "The Spirit of St. Louis Story." *Charles Lindbergh: An American Aviator*. http://www.charleslindbergh.com/hall/spirit.asp.

Maplecroft. "Maplecroft Food Security Index and interactive global map." *maplecroft.com*. May 21, 2008. maplecroft.com/about/news/Food_Security_Pressrelease.pdf.

"Minneapolis Bridge Collapse Kills 6." *FOXNews.com*. August 1, 2007. http://www.foxnews.com/story/0,2933,291790,00.html.

"Mosquito Information." *Survive Outdoors Inc.* http://
www.surviveoutdoors.com/reference/mosquito.asp.

"Number of births, birth rate, and percentage of births to
unmarried women: United States, 1940-2007." *CDC.
gov.* National Center for Health Statistics, National
Vital Statistics System. 2008. http://www.cdc.gov/
nchs/data/databriefs/db18_Fig_1.png.

Organization for Economic Cooperation and
Development. "An International Education Test."
New York Times. December 7, 2010. http://
www.nytimes.com/imagepages/2010/12/ 07/
education/07education_graph.html?ref=education.

Paine, Thomas. "The Crisis, by Thomas Paine, December
23, 1776." *USHistory.org.* Independence Hall
Association. http://www.ushistory.org/paine/
crisis/c-01.htm.

Philippines: Environment Monitor. "State of Water:
Philippines." *Water Environment Partnership in Asia.*
2003. http://www.wepa-db.net/policies/state/
philippines/overview.htm.

Randell, Shirley K., and Diana R. Gergel. "The Education
of Girls in Africa." *International Federation of University
Women.* Federation of University Women of Africa.
July 2009. http://www.ifuw.org/fuwa/docs/
Education_of_Girls_Africa.pdf.

Safeco Corp. "Safeco Survey Finds Small-Business
Owners Ill-Prepared To Recover Payroll, Expenses
and Profits When Disaster Strikes." *ICR.* October
21, 2003. http://www.icrsurvey.com/Study.
aspx?f=Safeco_1003.html.

Savage, Charlie. "Sex, Drug Use and Graft Cited in
Interior Department." *The New York Times.* September
10, 2008. http://www.nytimes.com/2008/09/11/
washington/11royalty.html?_r=2.

Shore, Rima and Barbara Shore. "KIDS COUNT Indicator Brief: Increasing the Percentage of Children Living in Two-Parent Families." *Annie E. Casey Foundation*. July 2009. http://www.aecf.org/~/media/Pubs/Initiatives/KIDS%20COUNT/K/Indicator Brief Increasing the Percentage/Two%20 Parent%20Families.pdf.

Spitzer, Eliot. "Did Goldman Lie to Congress? A damning new Senate report savages the Wall Street giant." *Slate Magazine*. April 25, 2011. http://www.slate.com/articles/news_and_politics/the_best_policy/2011/04/dont_let_goldman_off_the_hook.html.

"Tuition and Fees 2010-2011: Handbook for Students." *Harvard College*. http://isites.harvard.edu/icb/icb.do?keyword=k69286&tabgroupid=icb.tabgroup107418.

U.S. Department of Homeland Security. "FY 2011: Budget in Brief." *DHS.gov*. 2011. www.dhs.gov/xlibrary/assets/budget_bib_fy2011.pdf.

UNICEF. "Press centre - On Girls' Education and Poverty Eradication." *UNICEF.org*. July 15, 2003. http://www.unicef.org/media/media_11986.html.

Wilson, Scott, and Michael D. Shear. "Gen. McChrystal is dismissed as top U.S. commander in Afghanistan." *WashingtonPost.com*. June 24, 2010. http://www.washingtonpost.com/wp-dyn/content/article/2010/06/23/AR2010062300689.html?hpid=topnews&sid=ST2010062202674.

"A Year on, Gulf still grapples with BP oil spill." *Reuters.com*. April 19, 2011. http://www.reuters.com/article/2011/04/19/us-oil-spill-anniversary-idUSTRE73E2OW20110419.

References

Chapter 1. The nature of leadership

p. 15 – "*...that battle won us a nation.*": David McCullough. *1776*. New York: Simon & Schuster, 2005.

pp. 16-17 – "*We were born free...to die free is an obligation.*": This old adage is used by patriotic, right-thinking Americans who understand that freedom isn't free, and that with freedom comes responsibility.

p. 18 – "*...of whom nearly a million are in the military.*": "Korea Average Salary Income - Job Comparison." *WorldSalaries.org*. 2005. http://www.worldsalaries.org/korea.shtml.

Chapter 2. The first 3 lessons of leadership

p. 28 – "*...leaders must inspire people to willingly follow.*": Theodore Levitt. "Marketing Myopia." *Harvard Business Review*. July-August, 2004. http:/hbr.org/2004/07/marketing-myopia/ar/1?referral=00269.

Chapter 3. The New Normal

p. 36 – "*Galileo proclaimed the idea...*": Maurice A. Finocchiaro. "Chronology of Events." In *The Galileo Affair: A Documentary History*, by Galileo Galilei, pp. 297-308. Berkeley: University of California Press, 1989.

p. 37 – "*...two days for him to lose his job.*": Scott Wilson and Michael D. Shear. "Gen. McChrystal is dismissed as top U.S. commander in Afghanistan." *WashingtonPost.com*. June 24, 2010. http://www.washingtonpost.com/wp-dyn/content/article/2010/06/23/

AR2010062300689.html?hpid=topnews&sid= ST2010062202674.

p. 38 – "...*Paris houses 63,320 per square mile.*": Vikki Campion. "Sydney city crams its people in with higher population than London, Paris." *Herald Sun.* April 20, 2011. http://www.heraldsun.com.au/ news/victoria/sydney-city-crams-its-people-in/story-e6frf7l6-1226041915800.

p. 39 – "...*one million people homeless...*": "Haiti." *The New York Times.* August 16, 2012. http:// topics.nytimes.com/top/news/international/ countriesandterritories/haiti/index.html.

p. 47 – "...*well-cared-for on Main Street?*": Alan Bjerga. "Food Stamp Recipients at Record 41.8 Million Americans in July, U.S. Says." *Bloomberg.* October 5, 2010. http://www.bloomberg.com/news/2010-10-05/food-stamp-recipients-at-record-41-8-million-americans-in-july-u-s-says.html.

p. 47 – "...*$90,000 per death row inmate every year.*": Death Penalty Information Center. "Costs of Death Penalty." *DeathPenaltyInfo.org.* 2012. http://www. deathpenaltyinfo.org/costs-death-penalty.

p. 47 – "...*Harvard University for a year.*": "Tuition and Fees 2010-2011 Handbook for Students 2010-2011." *Harvard College.* 2010. http://isites.harvard. edu/icb/icb.do?keyword=k69286&tabgroupid=icb. tabgroup107418.

p. 48 – On the virtual predestination of some children to a life that involves prison time: "Cradle to Prison Pipeline Campaign." *Children's Defense Fund.* 2012. http:// www.childrensdefense.org/programs-campaigns/ cradle-to-prison-pipeline/index.html.

Chapter 4. The global environment

p. 63 – "*...doctors and well-diggers.*": Angus Deaton interview by Jennifer Robison. "News Flash: Money Does Buy Happiness." *Gallup Business Journal.* Jan. 2008.

p. 67-70 – *Ghana success story.*: "Ghana: Nation at 55 – Poised for a Great Leap Forward?" *allAfrica.* March 9, 2012. http://allafrica.com/stories/201203091485.html.

p. 69 – "*...parts of the Asian model and parts of the U.S. model.*": With the Asian model, rice is grown on small farms and farmers process the rice in local cooperatives; they leave with bags of processed rice for home use, while the rest is sold to a wholesaler. With the U.S. model, the farms are 2,000 to 3,000 acres and most or all of the rice is sold to a processing company.

p. 71 – "*...equal education for boys and girls...*": Around the world, countries that offer girls the same educational opportunities as boys are more economically sound and politically stable. This has been clearly demonstrated in African countries. (Grace Chibiko Offorma. *Girl-Child Education in Africa.* July 2009. http://www.ifuw.org/fuwa/docs/Education of Girls Africa.pdf.)

p. 71 – "*...Asian-American and Pacific-Islander children.*": Rima Shore and Barbara Shore. "KIDS COUNT Indicator Brief: Increasing the Percentage of Children Living in Two-Parent Families." *Annie E. Casey Foundation.* July 2009. http://www.aecf.org/~/media/Pubs/Initiatives/KIDS%20COUNT/K/Indicator Brief Increasing the Percentage/Two%20Parent%20Families.pdf.

pp. 71-72 – *Unmarried mothers*.: "Number of births, birth rate, and percentage of births to unmarried women: United States, 1940-2007." *CDC.gov*. National Center for Health Statistics, National Vital Statistics System. 2008. http://www.cdc.gov/nchs/data/databriefs/db18_Fig_1.png.

pp. 74-75 – *AIDS*.: "AIDS Timeline." *AVERT.org*. http://www.avert.org/aids-timeline.htm.

Chapter 5. Your job is now your mission

pp. 80-81 – *Eastern Seaboard snowstorm*.: Sean Gregory. "Cory Booker: The Mayor of Twitter and Blizzard Superhero." *TIME.com*. December 29, 2010. http://www.time.com/time/nation/article/0,8599,2039945,00.html.

p. 91 – *"...didn't manage perceptions so well."*: George W. Bush. *Decision Points*. New York: Crown Publishers, 2010.

p. 96 – *"...emergency kit from the Red Cross..."*: Lt. Gen. Russel L. Honoré (U.S. Army, Ret.) with Ron Martz. *Survival: How a Culture of Preparedness Can Save You and Your Family From Disasters*. New York: Atria Books, 2009.

p. 97 – *"...do what we ought to do."*: Andrew Dunn. "New regulations could reduce mosquito abatement programs." *StarNewsOnline.com*. March 17, 2011. http://www.starnewsonline.com/article/ 20110317/ARTICLES/110319675.

Chapter 6. Decision superiority

pp. 102-104 – *Bill Gates story.*: "History of Windows: Highlights from the first 25 years." *Microsoft Windows.* http://windows.microsoft.com/en-US/windows/history.

p. 109 – "*...including their own customers.*": Eliot Spitzer. "Did Goldman Lie to Congress? A damning new Senate report savages the Wall Street giant." *Slate Magazine.* April 25, 2011. http://www.slate.com/articles/news_and_politics/the_best_policy/2011/04/dont_let_goldman_off_the_hook.html.

p. 111 – "*...400,000 homes were lost as a result of that storm.*": Brian Kurpis. *Hurricane Katrina Relief.* http://www.hurricanekatrinarelief.com/.

pp. 111, 114-115 – *BP oil spill and MMS "dearth of regulations.":* Mark Clayton. "BP oil spill: MMS shortcomings include 'dearth of regulations.'" The *Christian Science Monitor.* June 17, 2010. http://www.csmonitor.com/USA/Politics/2010/0617/BP-oil-spill-MMS-shortcomings-include-dearth-of-regulations.

Chapter 7. The true purpose of business

p. 119 – "*...American business looks bad.*": ABC News. "International flights forced to wait on tarmac overnight at JFK Airport." *ABClocal.go.com.* December 28, 2010. http://abclocal.go.com/wabc/story?section=weather&id=7866145.

p. 120 – "*...failure of the quicker-and-cheaper paradigm.*": Anita Campbell. "Business Failure Rates Highest in First Two Years." *Small Business Trends.* July 7, 2005. http://smallbiztrends.com/2005/07/business-failure-rates-highest-in.html.

p. 123 - *"...base of faithful customers is a life-or-death matter for every business."*: Levitt, Theodore. "Marketing Myopia." *Harvard Business Review.* July-August, 2004. http:/hbr.org/2004/07/marketing-myopia/ar/1?referral=00269.

p. 127 - *"...40 percent of small businesses crash within five years of one."*: Safeco Corp. "Safeco Survey Finds Small-Business Owners Ill-Prepared To Recover Payroll, Expenses and Profits When Disaster Strikes." *ICR.* October 21, 2003. http://www.icrsurvey.com/Study.aspx?f=Safeco_1003.html.

Chapter 8. Earning your subordinates' loyalty and investing in their success

p. 134 - *"...only if they have good leadership."*: Alec M. Gallup and Frank Newport. *The Gallup Poll: Public Opinion 2006.* Lanham, Maryland: Rowman & Littlefield Publishers, 2007.

p. 138 - *"...pick your closest followers very carefully."*: Maj. Gen. Aubrey "Red" Newman (Ret.). *Follow Me: The Human Element in Leadership.* Novato, California: Presidio Press, 1981.

Chapter 9. Save your best leadership for when you get home

p. 162 - *"...you succeed at the most important responsibility you have."*: Dan Gediman, John Gregory, and Mary Jo Gediman. *This I Believe: On Fatherhood.* San Francisco: Jossey-Bass, 2011.

Index

Note: Page numbers in *Italic* refer to illustrations,
maps, and photographs

LT. GEN. RUSSEL L. HONORÉ (U.S. Army, retired) served in the military for 37 years. He led the U.S. Dept. of Defense response to Hurricanes Katrina and Rita in 2005 and was a commanding general in the Middle East and in Korea.

He served in a variety of command and staff positions focused on Defense Support of Civil Authorities and Homeland Defense.

A highly decorated soldier, he received numerous awards and medals, including the Defense Distinguished Service Medal, Legion of Merit, Bronze Star, Global War on Terrorism Service Medal and Kuwait Liberation Medal.

Today he is a business consultant, public speaker, Senior Scientist for the Gallup Organization, and CNN contributor on topics related to disaster preparedness. He holds a B.S. Degree in Vocational Agriculture from Southern University and an M.A. in Human Resources from Troy State. A native of Lakeland, Louisiana, he and his wife Beverly live in Baton Rouge, and they have four grown children.

———————•••• •———————

JENNIFER ROBISON is a Senior Editor for *The Gallup Business Journal*. A prolific author, she has written or co-written seven books and hundreds of magazine articles. She lives with her family in Crete, Nebraska.

Inspiring Books
from
Acadian House Publishing

Leadership in the New Normal

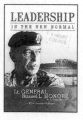

A 184-page hardcover book on how to be an effective leader in the 21st century. It describes modern leadership principles and techniques and illustrates them with stories from the author's life experiences. He emerged as a national hero and one of the U.S.'s best-known military leaders in 2005 after spearheading the post-Hurricane Katrina search-and-rescue mission in New Orleans. (Author: General Russel Honore. ISBN: 0-925417-81-5. Price $16.95)

Getting Over the 4 Hurdles of Life

A 160-page hardcover book that shows us ways to get past the obstacles, or hurdles, that block our path to success, happiness and peace of mind. This inspiring book – by one of the top motivational speakers in the U.S. – is brought to life by intriguing stories of various people who overcame life's hurdles. (Author: Coach Dale Brown. ISBN: 0-925417-72-6. Price $17.95)

Dreaming Impossible Dreams
Reflections of an Entrepreneur

This 176-page autobiography is the rags-to-riches story of multimillionaire philanthropist E.J. Ourso of Donaldsonville, Louisiana, the man for whom the LSU Business School is named. It reveals how Ourso acquired 56 businesses in 48 years – the first 25 with no money down. A testament to the effectiveness of the American free enterprise system, the book chronicles Ourso's life beginning with his early years as a salesman. It reveals his secrets to the acquisition of wealth. (Author: E.J. Ourso with Dan Marin. Softcover ISBN: 0-925417-43-2, Price $14.95)

The Forgotten Hero of My Lai
The Hugh Thompson Story

A 248-page hardcover book that tells the story of the U.S. Army helicopter pilot who risked his life to rescue South Vietnamese civilians and to put a stop to the My Lai massacre during the Vietnam War in 1968. An inspiring story about the courage to do the right thing under extremely difficult circumstances, regardless of the consequences. Illustrated with maps and photos. (Author: Trent Angers. ISBN: 0-925417-33-5. Price: $22.95)

TO ORDER, list the books you wish to purchase along with the corresponding cost of each. Add $4 per book for shipping & handling. Louisiana residents add 8% tax to the cost of the books. Mail your order and check or credit card authorization (VISA/MC/AmEx) to: Acadian House Publishing, Dept. B-72, P.O. Box 52247, Lafayette, LA 70505. Or call (800) 850-8851. To order online, go to www.acadianhouse.com.